From the Theorems

From the Theorems of Master Jean de La Ceppède

LXX SONNETS

a bilingual edition
selected and translated
with an introduction and notes by
KEITH BOSLEY

MID NORTHUMBERLAND ARTS GROUP
& CARCANET NEW PRESS

Acknowledgements

086 980

Keith Bosley was a finalist of the EEC Translation Competition organized by the publishers 1979-80.

Some of the translations in this book first appeared in the translator's *And I Dance* (1972), in *Agenda*, *The Jewish Quarterly*, and *Twofold*. Some have been broadcast on the BBC World Service.

The translator acknowledges the financial assistance of the Arts Council of Great Britain.

The Mid Northumberland Arts Group, the area arts association for central Northumberland, is sponsored by Wansbeck District Council in association with Northumberland Technical College, administered by the Leisure and Publicity Department of Wansbeck District Council, and grant-aided by Northern Arts.

PQ
1628
·L234
F76
1983

Published by Mid Northumberland Arts Group, Leisure & Publicity Department, Town Hall, Ashington, Northumberland NE63 8RX and Carcanet New Press, 208-210 Corn Exchange, Manchester M4 3BG.

ISBN 0 904790 26 6 (Mid Northumberland Arts Group)
ISBN 0 85635 450 3 (Carcanet New Press)

Set printed and bound in Great Britain by Billing & Sons Ltd, Worcester

Jean de La Ceppède
repented in psalms
and wrote theorems
to demonstrate God

his heavenly muse
faithful to the love
that at one remove
was death to the Jews:

reading his sonnets
the eye contemplates
a stained glass window

making dogma dance
as leaded lines show
a winged radiance.

                    K.B.

Table

THEOREMES

Premiere Partie (1613)

Premier Liure: la sortie de Ierusalem, la prinse de nostre Seigneur Iesus-Christ, & tout ce qui aduint au jardin d'Oliuet.

Second Liure: son retour en la ville, le procez fait, tant par les Pontifes, que par les Iuges lays, tout ce qu'on luy fit & qui arriua ceste nuict, & sa condemnation.

Contents

THEOREMS

First Part (1613)

First Book: the departure from Jerusalem, the taking of our Lord Jesus Christ, and all that came to pass in the garden of the Mount of Olives.

Second Book: his return to the city, the trial, by the high priests as well as by the lay judges, all that was done to him and took place that night, and his condemnation.

vii

Troisieme Liure: l'execution de sa cruele Sentence, & tout ce qui se passa au Mont de Caluaire.

Seconde Partie (1622)

Premier Liure: la descente de IESVS-CHRIST aux Enfers, & sa Resurrection.

Third Book: the carrying out of his cruel sentence, and all that happened on the hill of Calvary.

Second Part (1622)

First Book: the descent of Jesus Christ into hell, and his Resurrection.

Introduction

Black, yes, but you are fair, a prodigy
Of Nature, fairer than Love's fairest girl.
Dawn beside you is dark: your ebony
Casts into gloom both ivory and pearl . . .

Oh make thy selfe with holy mourning blacke,
And red with blushing, as thou art with sinne;
Or wash thee in Christs blood, which hath this might
That being red, it dyes red soules to white . . .

The pink was well content to bear eclipse
from the reflecting mouth, when in the rush
of its own modesty it raised a blush
and saw itself more like your ruby lips . . .

O Christ, O holy Lamb, I beg you, hold
All my red sins, these kindling-twigs of hell
Hid in your flesh's robe's each bloody fold . . .

A Baroque fanfare, a symphony in black, white and red – the Italian
poet Marino praising a Nubian slave girl, the English poet Donne
addressing his soul, the Spanish poet Quevedo reflecting on what
happened when his lady took a carnation between her teeth and bit
her lip, the French poet La Ceppède praying that his sins may be
literally blotted out (the translations are mine). All four poets were
flourishing around 1600, when European artists in all media were
questioning the values and conventions of the Renaissance. Nature
was giving way to artifice (hence Marino's interest in a 'prodigy'),
techniques were being stretched (hence the term Mannerism
applied to some early Baroque art), new forms (like opera) were
emerging. All this was taking place against a background of
religious wars as the Reformation met the Counter-Reformation
head on: no wonder modern European taste has swung towards the
Baroque.

The word Baroque began life, like most of the terms applied to the arts of the period, as a term of disapproval: it seems to have been borrowed by art historians from the language of Portuguese jewellers, who used it to denote a pearl of irregular shape. A Baroque poem too is a gem with unexpected highlights. The dominant theme of Baroque poetry is love, both human and divine; and Baroque poets cheerfully shift from one to the other without any change of tone, which is a blend of passionate feeling and strenuous thought. For Marino, black is beautiful, more beautiful than the white skin of his lady whose slave the girl is. For Donne, black is sin and penitence, red is sin and shame; but red is also Jesus' blood, which whitens. For Quevedo, red is a carnation, his lady's lips, and her blood; the carnation blushes with shame at her mouth, which prompts the lady – not to be outdone – to bite her lip, and the scene dissolves in tears and laughter. For La Ceppède, red is Jesus' purple robe, Eucharistic wine producing crimson tears and bloodstained poems, then his own sins, to be hidden in the robe of Jesus' flesh. Sometimes Baroque poets deliberately blur the distinction between sacred and profane: Donne, again, says that the Church, the spouse of Christ, 'is most trew . . . when she'is embrac'd and open to most men', and the later Polish poet Jan Andrzej Morsztyn – who translated Marino – asks to be crucified on the cross his lady is wearing; 'no wonder bodies rise from graves', he mischievously says, when the cross is 'set . . . between two thieves'.

This kind of metaphor and simile is called a conceit, in the sense of the Italian *concetto* 'concept'. Today the English word has narrowed to refer only to a man's exaggerated notion of himself, rather as another famous Baroque word, wit, has come to mean little more than a sense of humour. There is exaggeration too in the Baroque conceit, as the poet exercises his ingenuity, his wit, to connect the unconnected. To invoke Donne once more: in a world where lovers and cosmographers had little in common, he calls his lady his 'more then Moone' and implores her 'draw not up seas to drowne me in thy spheare', and on a happier day he likens himself and her to a pair of compasses growing erect as they approach each other. Such way-out connections were not new: a century and a half before, the Catalan poet Ausiàs March was comparing his well-ordered lady with the government of Venice and his helplessness before her with a Basque who falls ill in Germany. But between the conceit and the creativity, as it were, fell the shadow of Renaissance convention, and lovers were confined to their bowers and glades, visited only by zephyrs and nightingales. The famous 'Renaissance man' was a polymath, but he stacked his culture in separate piles: the gods of Olympus had little contact with the God of Sinai. It is customary to regard the Baroque as marking the decline of the Renaissance: well, in Renaissance terms it was, but from the viewpoint of the 20th century it can be seen as a fulfilment, at least in poetry. The world was expanding, but it was also becoming more complicated, and the many interests of Renaissance man were threatening to fragment him into as many pieces. The Baroque poet strove to hold the pieces together by making all things grist to his mill: to his contemporaries he was literally unconventional, even – as we would say – schizoid; but it was they who were schizoid, and it was he who recognised the condition and sought a remedy. Sometimes he succeeded; sometimes he over-prescribed, like Crashaw who, recalling the motion of the earth, presents the weeping eyes of St Mary Magdalen as 'two walking Baths, two weeping motions; / Portable and compendious Oceans'. But such motions are never far, in the Baroque world, from emotions: while we may find Baroque poetry more congenial than our Romantic forebears did, we still respond more to the wit of its conceits than to the driving force behind the wit. Many of us were brought up on Milton's recipe 'simple, sensuous and passionate' (*Of Education*) – evidence that in England by the mid-17th century taste was moving away from the Baroque. For Baroque poetry is certainly not simple, but it is no less sensuous and passionate: it is a poetry of the whole man (and woman, when we remember the Mexican poet Sor Juana) calling on a wide range of experience, like Vaughan comparing human restlessness with the movement of a shuttle on a loom, or Marvell likening ill-fated lovers to parallel lines which 'though infinite can never meet' – how poignant is that last word!

In the course of the 17th century the smoke of war cleared to reveal a new Classical age, beneath whose fresh certainties the worryings of the Baroque were to degenerate into the whimsy of Rococo. In 1693 Dryden accused Donne of 'affecting the metaphysics' and of 'perplexing the minds of the fair sex with nice speculations of philosophy when he should engage their hearts'. Dr Johnson took up the cry later, and the term Metaphysical poetry was born. It is singularly inappropriate: there is little poetry more physical than the Baroque variety. Some modern scholars have tried to dignify the term with an international meaning to contrast with Baroque, describing that as normative (its conceits always make sense) and this as not; others prefer to regard Metaphysical as the English term – where the Spaniards speak of *gongorismo* (after Góngora) and the Italians of *marinismo* (after Marino) or *secentismo* ('17th-century-ism') – and Baroque as the international term. Throughout Europe since the 17th century, Baroque poetry has had a rough ride, but nowhere rougher than in France. *Enfin Malherbe vint*, 'at last Malherbe came', the French still say, quoting their Classical poet Boileau: it was Malherbe who in the early 17th century was already laying the foundations of Classical taste,

3

rejecting the irregularities of the Renaissance and the excesses of his contemporaries. These included drawing-room poets known as *précieux* (a two-edged term like 'precious' in English) who were later to be satirised by Molière. D'Aubigné, the epic poet of the Protestant cause, was forgotten until the Romantics rediscovered him; but a worse fate befell several major Baroque poets like Sponde, Chassignet, and Malherbe's friend La Ceppède. When the first part of his *Theorems* appeared, Malherbe commended it to its royal patron Queen Marie de Médicis with a sonnet. When the second part was published, he was less enthusiastic:

Muses, vous promettez en vain
Au front de ce grand Escriuain
Et du laurier & du lierre.
Ses ouurages trop precieux
Pour les couronnes de la terre
L'asseurent de celle des cieux.

Muses, you vainly vow
That this great writer's brow
Shall wear a wreath of bay.
No earthly crown is given
For works so precious: they
Must wait for one in heaven.

Malherbe did his work well: his successors consigned La Ceppède to total oblivion, till he was unearthed by Henri Bremond in the first volume (1915) of his *Histoire littéraire du Sentiment religieux en France* (*Literary History of Religious Feeling in France*). Since then the poet has appeared in several anthologies – though not yet in *The Oxford Book of French Verse*; selections have been edited by Jean Rousset (*Jean de La Ceppède*, Paris 1947) and François Ruchon (*Essai sur la Vie et l'Œuvre de Jean de La Ceppède / Essay on the Life and Work of Jean de La Ceppède*, Geneva 1953), and in 1966 an expensive facsimile of the *Theorems* was published in Geneva. The only book about him is *The Poetry of Jean de La Ceppède: a study in text and context* by P.A.Chilton (Oxford 1977). The present selection should at least satisfy the curiosity of Dr Chilton's readers: it is the only popular edition of the poet in print.

Les Theoremes de Messire Iean de la Ceppede, Seigneur d'Aigalades, Cheualier, Conseiller du Roy en ses Conseils d'Estat & Priué, & premier President en sa Cour des Comptes, Aides, & Finances de Prouence, sur le sacré Mystere de nostre Redemption (The Theorems of Master Jean de La Ceppède, Lord of the Manor of Les Aygalades, Knight, King's Counsel in his State and Privy Councils, and first President in his Audit Office, Board of

4

Excise, and Exchequer of Provence, on the sacred Mystery of our Redemption) was published in Toulouse in 1613; the *Seconde Partie . . . sur les Mysteres de la descente de Iesus-Christ aux Enfers, de sa Resurrection, &c. (on the Mysteries of Jesus Christ's descent into Hell, of his Resurrection, etc.*) followed in 1622. La Ceppède was a *messire* – a master lawyer – a King's man and a devout Catholic. He was born in Marseille about 1548 into a family of Spanish origin which may have produced St Teresa of Avila (she was born a Cepeda), and he grew up in a period of religious turmoil whose bloodiest episode was the massacre of Protestants on the eve of the feast of St Bartholomew (whose emblem is a butcher's knife) in 1572. As a young man he was caught up in the 'War of the Three Henries': these were Henri III of France, Henry of Navarre the leader of the Huguenots, and Henri de Guise who in 1576 formed the *Sainte Ligue* – the Holy League – to defend the French throne against a Protestant succession. At this time the poet belonged to a royalist literary circle which included the son of Nostradamus, and he was beginning to write the *Theorems*. Over the next ten years the *Ligue* made gains in a Provence already in secessionist mood with a linguistic and cultural revival, culminating in the takeover in 1586 of the Parliament of Aix-en-Provence, of which the poet was a prominent member. In 1589 he was arrested; he tried to escape disguised as a shoemaker, was shot and recaptured, but freed on the instructions of a *Ligue* member who held him in high regard. In the same year Henry of Navarre became Henri IV of France, and in 1593 he embraced the Catholic faith with the famous remark *Paris vaut bien une messe* – 'Paris is well worth a Mass'. 1594 saw the poet's first published work, an 'imitation' of the Seven Penitential Psalms; it was one of many peace-offerings by poets of Provence as France was reunified. In 1596 Marseille fell to the King, who in 1598 promulgated the Edict of Nantes, guaranteeing civil rights and freedom of worship to the Huguenots, and in 1600 the poet made a speech of welcome to the Queen. It was to her, as Queen Mother, that he dedicated the first part of the *Theorems*; by this time (1613) Henri IV had been assassinated by a Jesuit agent, and the throne had passed to his small son Louis XIII. The poet sent a copy of his book to St Francis de Sales, Bishop of Geneva, who declared himself *attiré par cette sçavante piété qui vous fait si heureusement transformer les muses payennes en chrestiennes* – 'drawn by that learned piety which so happily makes you transform the pagan muses into Christian ones'. The second part of the *Theorems* was dedicated to Louis XIII, celebrating his coming of age with a visit to Provence after defeating the Protestants of Languedoc. La Ceppède died, full of years and honours, in Avignon in July 1623. The following year Cardinal Richelieu, the *éminence grise*, became prime minister; the Golden Age began; and our poet was forgotten.

Theōrēma is a Greek word meaning a spectacle, an object of study; hence, in mathematics, a demonstration of a truth not self-evident. To La Ceppède the truths of the Catholic faith were to be visualised

5

(a favourite expression of his is *peinture parlante* – 'talking picture' – and in one sonnet he uses a word from the language of painters) and, with the help of the heavenly muse Urania, proved. 'Except demonstrations (and perchance there are very few of them) I find nothing without perplexities', Donne wrote in a letter to an unnamed correspondent in 1613: we shall never know whether this Catholic turned Protestant, with his 'immoderate desire of humane learning and languages', was referring to a Catholic poet's 'demonstrations' published in the same year. Readers of Donne will find La Ceppède not at all perplexed: perhaps his nearest English equivalent is the George Herbert of the tremendous sonnet 'Prayer the Churches banquet'. The *Theorems* is a colossal work running to over 1200 pages: it consists of 520 sonnets, each accompanied by a commentary which varies in length from three lines to twenty-seven pages. Each sonnet, according to the author, is a meditation: the First Part is in three Books of 100 sonnets each, plus a sonnet headed *Vœu pour la fin de cet Œuvre* – 'Prayer to end this Work'; the Second Part is in four Books of 50, 100, 35 and 30 sonnets respectively, plus a 'prayer' sonnet at the end of each Book. The primary sources are the last three chapters of Matthew, Mark and Luke, the last four of John, and the first two of Acts; the secondary sources are passages in the Hebrew Bible – the Old Testament – to which Christianity claims a complement in the New, and the writings of Church Fathers. As the poet points out in his 'Foreword: To France' (extracts from which precede the present selection) he is strictly orthodox, and he prefers earlier authorities to later; some readers have detected in his vivid evocations the influence of the *Spiritual Exercises* of St Ignatius Loyola, but the poet does not mention the founder of the order that dispatched his king. Like an icon painter, he claims no credit for his images and symbols, seeing his role purely as an arranger of received material.

The selection opens with a sonnet that puts the Renaissance muse in her place (*1:1:6* – such references are to Part, Book and Sonnet). The poet soon 'transforms' her: in *1:1:96* Jesus is a Hercules, in *1:3:18* his Cross disturbs Hades, in *1:3:20* he is an Orpheus rescuing the Eurydice of the soul, in *1:3:22* he is a Deucalion, the Greek Noah. Christian typology makes its first appearance with *1:1:21* as a parallel is drawn between Rachel dying after giving birth to Benjamin and Jesus dying in order to give birth to the Church. This interpretative tradition brings out elsewhere the antisemitism endemic in a religion that sees itself as the inheritor of a covenant forfeited by its founder's own nation: in *1:1:96* the Jews fail to recognise a cosmic Samson, in *1:2:72* they pollute Jesus' divinity as Reuben polluted his father's bed, in *1:2:73* they kill a latter-day Solomon, in *1:2:85* they repeat an ancestral error... and so on; they are also the bad guys in the powerful blow-by-blow accounts of Jesus' arrest, torture, trial and execution. But this is only one aspect of the *Theorems*; there are many others, such as in the sonnets which draw on the world of nature – the need to stoop in order to drink both from a stream on a hot day and from the waters of eternal life (*1:1:29*), the disciples seen as birds (*1:1:79*), Jesus the gardener (*1:1:99*), the dignity of the humble reed (*1:2:65*), the tree of the Cross in which human affections build nests (*1:3:30*), the Resurrection likened to the metamorphosis of the silkworm (*2:1:26*).

The Baroque conceit comes into its own in sonnets like *1:1:38*, where Jesus in Gethsemane 'moves aside' from his divinity to suffer as a man, and his sweat is likened to the juice of a grape being crushed; the similes in *1:1:48* are boldly transposed as the poet, instead of comparing Judas with owls and desert, describes Judas and then compares owls and desert with each other; in *1:1:88* he prays to be freed from worldly distractions as the young man in Mark 14 escaped arrest by slipping out of his clothes. Unique in the whole work is the pair of sonnets *1:2:67* and *68*, which use the same rhymes – sometimes even the same rhyme-words – and both end with the same word: in *67* Jesus' tortures make him look like a leper, in *68* the poet prays to be cleansed from the leprosy of sin. Perhaps the most remarkable conceit is in *1:2:71*, the third sonnet of an *Ecce homo* triptych, where Jesus hides his divinity under human flesh as Rachel sat on her father's idols and pleaded menstruation.

Part 3 of Book 1 is the heart of the *Theorems* – the crucifixion, death and burial. According to Dr Chilton, these sonnets were the first to be written; some may go back to the late 1570s, when the poet was about thirty. Here is 'the mind at the tips of the senses' as he confronts the horror. Jesus is flayed alive when his robe is torn off (*10*); he is stretched on the Cross as on a rack (*16*); the magnificent sequence *18-31* takes us from the sounds of the crucifixion – the thud of wood against rock, sobs, whispers, screams, shouts – to the Cross dominating the sky on the last day. Book 3 ends with a *Pietà* group in which, interestingly, the central figure is St Mary Magdalen: in her lamentation (*98*) she springs to credible life as she reveals that she is as sorry for herself as she is for Jesus. Soon after this the La Ceppède Passion ends; for its range and depth it is reminiscent of the Passions of another once neglected provincial genius, J.S.Bach.

Western Christendom has filled its churches with images of the suffering Jesus; for Christ the Lord of all we must turn to the domes and cupolas of the East. But La Ceppède is a Westerner, and henceforth he is largely on his own. For Book 1 of Part 2 even the New Testament narrative deserts him, and he must do what he can with the bald statements of the Creeds. 'He descended into hell': in *5* modern man has a vision of aircraft which modulates into the challenge of the Psalmist – 'Lift up your heads, O ye gates'. In many sonnets in Part 2 the poet ranges more widely than before: early natural history supplies Christ as the new phoenix (*2:1:35*), as a stag (*2:1:50* – though here there are biblical echoes too), as a whale (*2:2:64*); astrology shows Christ to be

7

master of the Zodiac (2:1:43). These are curiosities beside the beautiful 'prayer' sonnet which closes Book 1, a meditation on Christ as the new Hermes Trismegistus, radiating love like a gravitational field. When the New Testament narrative swims back into his ken, the poet finds much of it intractable, and Book 2, dealing with the appearances of the risen Christ, has more piety than poetry. The curve begins to sweep upward again in the much shorter Book 3, with the extraordinary Ascension sonnet (11) which likens Mary to a sunflower, and the visionary triumph sonnet (25) with its stained-glass fanfares and – at last – its presentation of Christ the Lord of all.

With Book 4 the poet is back in his stride for the last lap. According to Dr Chilton's chronology, these last sonnets are separated from the first by some forty years. For the first time, the old poet mentions himself by name as he prays for a final divine spark (1). The theme is Pentecost – wind and fire: the Holy Spirit is noisy, whereas Satan operates by stealth (6); the 'still small voice' was enough for Elijah, but we need to be shouted at (7); the tongues were divided like gifts, not cloven like those of snakes (9); their fire is the 'hot Gospel' (17). Pentecost reverses Babel, says the poet, repeating as always a traditional formula (23): we await the Second Coming.

Translating La Ceppède carries a special responsibility, since those who cannot read him in French have little opportunity to compare versions (the following Note on the Text is addressed to those who can). My only predecessors in English verse seem to be William Stirling, who published translations of two sonnets in From Machaut to Malherbe (London 1947), and Harold B. Segal, who has translated two in his book The Baroque Poem: a comparative survey (New York 1974); English prose versions can be found in Geoffrey Brereton's Penguin Book of French Verse, Part 2 and in Baroque Poetry edited by J.P.Hill and E.Caracciolo-Trejo (London and Totowa, New Jersey, 1975) – though the latter cannot be excused two elementary errors of translation. My only conscious liberties have been to harmonise tenses (the poet's narrative often switches for no good reason from a present tense in a main clause to a perfect tense in a subordinate clause), and to spell out cross-references to sonnets not translated. Unlike much Renaissance poetry, the 'strong lines' characteristic of the Baroque are full of particulars. When La Ceppède likens Mary to a flower with an unfamiliar name, any old flower will not do: the translator must hunt it down, arriving eventually at the sunflower which (by any other name) follows the sun as Mary's gaze follows the ascending Christ. This particularity led me in these sonnets to introduce new rhymes into the second quatrain, so that my sonnets have seven rhymes (like a Shakespeare sonnet) against the original five in a language which rhymes more readily anyway; otherwise, unlike Spenser translating Du Bellay, I have followed the original schemes, a heliotrope to La Ceppède's purple. Unlike most of his predecessors and contemporaries, he rhymes variously (and, alas, not always well) within the traditional limits: his only constants are a rhyme linking lines 4 and 5 of the octave (which I have not reproduced) and a couplet at the beginning of the sestet (which I have). The latter, a feature of the French sonnet, gives it the shape of a pot, whereas the Elizabethan sonnet, with its final tying-up couplet, is more like a parcel. Throughout the *Theorems* La Ceppède uses the twelve-syllable alexandrine, which occupies in French poetry a place similar to that of the iambic pentameter in English. Translating the one into the other I have come up against the usual problem: the French line is balanced, whereas the English line is not. Lacking stress, French poetry counts syllables rather than feet (and rather unhelpfully calls syllables 'feet') so rhythmic patterns can be perceived only if a line as long as the alexandrine is subdivided; the most satisfactory subdivision has been felt to be half way. One of the most rigorously balanced lines in the *Theorems* is *Son amour est si grand, son amour est si fort* (1:3:20): my translation – 'So great his love, his great love is so mighty' – demonstrates the English translator's problem. A literal version ('His love is so great, his love is so strong') would be preferred in many quarters today: the balance, the syllabic basis give a suggestion of 'making it new', in Pound's borrowed phrase, and in such a mood the translator would not bother about rhyme. I might have rendered the line thus myself if I had been translating this sonnet only, and if it had been well known; but translating a book of sonnets by a little-known poet one has other priorities. I hope that my translation 'makes it new' in more exciting ways, by using the asymmetry of the corresponding English line and achieving the more sophisticated satisfaction of some sort of rhyme. My concern throughout has been to produce the kind of 'strong lines' for which Baroque poets were once blamed and are now praised.

To himself, La Ceppède was a Renaissance poet who 'converted' the muse: in his Foreword he casts himself in the role of the prophet Hosea, and the muse in that of the harlot Gomer whom he married and from whom he begot Jezreel. Many of the poet's later countrymen have taken him too much at his word, seeing him somewhat as Gwilym in the Dylan Thomas story, who wrote poems to girls and then changed the girls' names to God. But we have Donne, Herbert, Crashaw, Vaughan: La Ceppède belongs in their company.

Over the fifteen years that I have lived with La Ceppède, many people have contributed insights to this book. The Rev. W. D. Kennedy-Bell gave seven sonnets the hospitality of a week's devotional programmes on the BBC World Service, which later, thanks to Mr John Pitman, rebroadcast one in my series *The Poetry of Europe*. The Rev. David Woodard shed light on an obscure reference. Dr Paul Chilton of Warwick University, the author of the only book on the poet, approved my labours (to my great relief) and supplied valuable information. Mr Anthony Rudolf monitored my progress and reassured me that our

Jewish friends would recognise a great Christian poet when they saw one.

Keith Bosley
Upton-cum-Chalvey 1981

Note on the Text

The French text is that of the first edition, published in the poet's lifetime (Part I in 1613, Part II in 1622, not reprinted until the facsimile edition of 1966), incorporating corrections from the 1613 list of *errata*; a few obvious misprints have been silently corrected. Two conventions have been modernised: the long *s*, and the abbreviated nasal, whereby *m* or *n* following a vowel in the same syllable was occasionally reduced to a horizontal stroke over the vowel (*rayõ*). The original punctuation has on the whole been preserved; where it is lacking or misleading, the translation attempts to clarify. The layout is modern, replacing the original indentations with line spaces.

Renaissance spelling, in French as in English, does not distinguish *i* from *j*, or *u* from *v*. Of the former pair, *i* serves for both (*iardin*, *Iuif*), though the poet's printer slips in the odd *j*, and capital *J* is sometimes used for variety (*Jl*, *Jsraël*). Of the latter pair, *v* is used in capitals and at the beginning of words (*IESVS*, *vn*), *u* elsewhere (*rauage*, *vniuers*); vocalic *u* is sometimes marked with diaeresis (*coüarde*, *deüe*). Spelling often tries to reflect etymology at the expense of pronunciation (*nostre* from *nostrum*, though long since pronounced *notre*; *seur* from *securum*, though pronounced *sûr*); sometimes it tries too hard (*sçavoir* is not from *scire*, but from *sapere). Diacritics are mostly used to distinguish homophones (*à*, *dés*, *où*) and to mark a final acute *e* (*beauté*, *desiré*). The plural of these is usually spelt with *z*, which dispenses with the diacritic (*beautez*, *desirez*); conversely, *vous*-forms of verbs are occasionally spelt without *z* (*employés*). The use of diacritics was gaining ground: in adjoining lines of the same sonnet in 1613 *trespas* becomes *trépas*, and in 1622 *cette* is often spelt *céte*, though the poet's name is always spelt without a diacritic. His language also preserves features which had disappeared or were dying out further north: these are dealt with in the Notes at the back of the book.

Prosodically, the poet follows the Renaissance model of balanced alexandrines with alternating masculine and feminine rhymes, avoiding hiatus and enjambement. But French poetry has not yet said goodbye to everyday speech: reporting (or so it seems) the Crucifixion, he writes *elle a eu bel à teindre* (*1:3:16*), and when he uses enjambement the effect is literally breathtaking: in *S'escartant donc vn peu de sa maiestueuse / Et diuine grandeur* (*1:1:38*) we can almost see Jesus 'moving

11

aside'; in *Des citoyens du ciel plus que ie ne pourroy / Nombrer* (2:3:25) the poet is losing count of the blessed, and he resumes the line with a capital. One of the prosodic 'reforms' brought in by his Classical successors was that a 'mute' *e* could not follow a full vowel unless it was elided, as in Boileau's *génie inspiré*; so our poet was one of the last until modern times to use words like *tranchées* (1:1:21) and phrases like *qu'il en sue le sang* (1:1:38), where 'mute' *e* counts as a syllable.

Avant-Propos : A la France

EXTRAITS

Que l'enuieux reply des ans ride les beautez perissables, ce n'est pas grand merueille à ceux, qui par la iudicieuse raison discourent les œuures de la Nature. Mais que l'enuieux nuage du temps puisse ternir les beautez immorteles; c'est vn effect qui donne de l'admiration aux plus beaux esprits. Tes doctes nourrissons, ô docte France, qui ont foüillé curieusement dans les monumens de l'antiquité, sçauent que la Poësie a tenu le premier rang parmy les beautez non morteles & sainctes. Le fabuleux crayon des vieilles peintures parlantes nous a pourtrait ceste verité en mile & mile tableaux; tantost figurant cette Deesse naissante de Juppin & de Mnemosyne; tantost l'honorant de neuf diuers noms tous expressifs de ses diuerses perfections; tantost la montant sur l'Olympe; & tantost la faisant l'agreable compagne du bel Apollon. L'irreprochable tesmognage de ceux, qu'on estime auoir diuinement philosophé, appele les espris de la Poësie sacrez & diuins. Les sacrez honneurs, qu'elle a depuis tant de siecles immortalisé, nous tesmognent l'immortalité de ses graces: & l'Eternel (pour passer des ombres à la lumiere) nous fit iadis bien voir clairement combien il agreoit cette belle, luy faisant ores prononcer les arrests de sa volonté; ores entonner ses loüanges; ores rechanter ses bienfaits; ores croniquer la vie & les gestes de son fils bien-aymé. Toutesfois le retour des années la veüe du depuis si defformée, qu'à peine recognoissoit-on plus en elle rien de celeste, ny d'immortel; si qu'au lieu d'estre tousiours la mignonne du tout-Puissant, & de seruir à ses offices sacrez; elle estoit deuenue la seruante des hommes corrompus; & n'estoit plus employée qu'à l'adoration des feintes deitez; qu'à la menteuse flaterie, dont elle endormoit les grands vicieux au chant de leurs fauses loüanges; qu'au maquerelage des folastres & lasciues amours. Et bien que la molesse & la corruption de la plus grande partie de ceux qui l'ont possedée, luy eussent laissé croistre si longs les cheueux de l'Idolatrie, du mensonge, & de la volupté, qu'elle en fut tres-horrible; si l'auoient ils fardée si subtilement & si pompeusement parée, que facilement la peu caute ieunesse couroit apres ce masque trompeur, & se laissoit piper à cette amorce aleschante. I'en parle comme experimenté; car dés le plus tendre auril de mon âge affriandé de ses chatoüilleuses mignardises, ie la receus comme ma plus delicate delice; mais bien-tost apres (esclairé d'vn fauorable rayon du Soleil de Iustice) ie la demasqué, & recognu que celle, qui fut iadis fille du Ciel, estoit deuenue serue de l'Enfer, & que toutes ses premieres beautez estoient non seulement fanées, ains presque ruinées par l'hideuse laideur des vices; c'est pourquoy ie fus maintes fois sur le poinct de luy bailler le billet du repude & la chasser bien loin de moy: toutesfois me ressouuenant que ce grand Dieu tire bien quelque fois d'vne publique vne semence agreable: & permet aux siens de retenir, voire d'espouser vne estrangere & captiue pourueu qu'on la despoüille de ses vestemens prophanes, & qu'on luy rase le poil; ie prins resolution de l'arrester encore auecque moy, & de tenter si par ce mesme moyen ie pourroy restaurer ses anciennes beautez, la rendre d'esclaue libre, de Payenne Israëlite, & tirer encor d'elle vn Iezrahël. Or pour luy descoudre ses mondains habits (ou plustost habitudes) pour luy raire ses cheueux idolatres, menteurs & lascifs; i'aduisay qu'on ne pouuoit mettre en œuure vn outil plus vtile que le rasoir à double tranchant de la profonde meditation de la Passion & mort de nostre Sauueur IESVS-CHRIST: en quoy certes ie ne me trompay nullement; car des lors qu'elle se sentit seulement toucher de cest heureux cautere elle mesme deschira ses vieux habillemens, & s'arracha sa Medusine perruque. . . .

Cette Ethnique donques, ainsi repurgée & faite Chrestienne, commença bien-tost apres de conceuoir, non (comme auparauant) des auortons monstreux, mais des beaux enfans immortels, qu'elle a du depuis en diuerses ventrées enfantez au Seigneur. Desquels apres les embrasemens de nos derniers mal-heurs, i'ay fait naistre cettuy-cy, portant en sa main le liure du Prophete enuelopé des mysteres, escrit dedans pour les doctes, & dehors pour les ignorans . . .

I'ay creu qu'vn enfant si fructueux ne deuoit point estre retenu croupissant dans le cloistre de sa naissance: & pour ce (le seurant aussi-tost que i'ay peu), ie l'ay congedié de sortir au iour, pour se communiquer librement à tous, singulierement aux amoureux de sa Mere, & de la Pieté. Ie confesse que ie l'enuoye vn peu mal proprement habillé; non pour le regard de l'estoffe (car ie l'ay toute choisie dans les plus loyales boutiques des plus riches & plus fideles marchands de l'Eglise) mais quant à la façon des habits, qui ne sera peut-estre pas trouuée du tout bien à la Françoise; toutesfois ie me promets que ton naturel debonnaire excusera facilement ce defaut, & le rendra tres-excusable parmy les ames non enuieuses: consideré que ce fort drap d'or ne se manie pas aisément à tous les plis qu'on veut, & que nostre ramage natal ne peut facilement estre oublié tout à fait. Or pour ce que la calomnie, qui mord ordinairement sur nos actions, attaque principalement les œuures qui traittent de la religion, pour les arguer d'heresie, i'ay voulu moy-mesme faire des annotations à mes Theoremes, pour marquer les lieux de l'Escriture, ou des Saincts Peres qui me doiuent estre à garent de tout ce que i'ay escrit; que i'ay neantmoins sousmis & sousmets encore maintenant pour tousiours à la censure de l'Eglise: protestant de ne vouloir iamais insister qu'à ce qu'elle approuuera. . . .

Foreword : To France

That the invidious unfolding of the years should wrinkle perishable beauties, is no great wonder to those who by judicious reason hold forth the works of nature. But that the invidious mist of time may tarnish immortal beauties, is an effect that amazes the finest minds. Your learned scions, O learned France, who have in their curiosity rummaged among the monuments of antiquity, knows that Poetry has held pride of place amid beauties that are not mortal, that are holy. The fabled pencil of the old talking pictures has portrayed for us that truth in a myriad images, sometimes representing that goddess being born of Jove and Mnemosyne, sometimes honouring her with nine several names all expressive of her several perfections, sometimes raising her on Olympus, sometimes making her the acceptable companion of fair Apollo. The unimpeachable testimony of those whose philosophy is reckoned divine call the spirits of Poetry sacred and divine. The sacred honours which she has over so many centuries made immortal testify to us the immortality of her graces, and the Lord God (to pass from shadow to light) once clearly revealed to us how acceptable to him was this fair one, causing her now to pronounce the decrees of his will, now to hymn his praises, now to tell over his benefits, now to chronicle the life and deeds of his beloved Son. And yet the changing years have since then seen her so disfigured that anything heavenly or immortal could barely be recognised in her any more; indeed, that instead of being always the darling of the Almighty and performing his sacred offices, she had become the handmaid of corrupt men, and was no longer employed but to adore false deities, to flatter with lies and so lull great sinners by singing their wrongful praises, to play the bawd to wanton and lascivious loves. And though the softness and corruption of the greater part of those who possessed her had let her grow to such length the hair of idolatry, of untruth and of sensual pleasure, that she was made most horrible, indeed they had raddled her so subtly and so grandly adorned her, that without much ado unwary youth was running after this deceitful mask and letting itself be lured towards this tempting bait. I speak from experience, for from the tenderest April of my age enticed by her tickling caresses I received her as my most delicate delight; but soon afterwards, enlightened by a propitious beam from the Sun of righteousness,

I unmasked her and recognised that she who was once a daughter of heaven had become a slave of hell, and that all her pristine beauties were not only faded but wellnigh ruined by the foul ugliness of vices: that is why I was many times on the point of serving her with a bill of divorcement and driving her far away from me; mindful however that this great God oftentimes draws from a harlot an acceptable seed, and allows his own to keep, nay to marry, a foreigner and a captive provided she be stripped of her profane raiment and her head be shaved, I resolved to detain her with me and see whether by the same means I might not restore her former beauties, make her from a slave a freedwoman, from a pagan an Israelite, and draw yet from her a Jezreel. Now, to unstitch her worldly habits (in both senses of that word), to shave off her idolatrous, lying and lascivious hair, it occurred to me that no more useful tool could serve my purpose than the two-edged razor of profound meditation on the Passion and death of our Saviour Jesus Christ; wherein I was surely not at all deceived, for the moment she felt but the touch of this happy cautery she herself tore off her old apparel and snatched away her Medusa's wig. . . .

This gentile, then, thus purged and made Christian, began soon after to conceive, not (as before) monstrous freaks, but fair immortal children, whom she has since in several broods borne to the Lord. Of whom after the conflagrations of our late woes I have begotten this one, bearing in his hand the book of the Prophet wrapped in the mysteries, written within for the learned and without for the ignorant . . .

I have thought that such a fruitful child should not be kept wallowing in the cloister of his birth; and therefore, weaning him as soon as I could, I have given him leave to go out into the light of day to make himself freely available to all, especially to lovers of his Mother and of piety. I confess that I am sending him forth somewhat improperly dressed, not as regards the fabric (for I have chosen it all from the most loyal shops of the Church's richest and most faithful merchants) but as far as the style is concerned, which may not be found entirely *comme il faut*; I assure myself however that your good nature will readily excuse this shortcoming and that you will plead its case among souls who are not envious, bearing in mind that this tough cloth of gold is not easily coaxed into all the desired folds, and that our native twitter cannot readily be quite disregarded. Now, because slander, which commonly has its tooth in what we do, mainly attacks works which treat of religion, to accuse them of heresy, I have taken upon myself to add notes to my Theorems, to mark the places in Scripture or the Holy Fathers which must vouch for me in all that I have written, which I have nonetheless submitted and still submit now for ever to the Church's censure, affirming my wish never to assert but what she will approve. . . .

Premiere Partie
Premier Liure

First Book
First Part

[6]

Prophanes Amphions qui n'employés la Muse
Qu'à chanter d'Helicon les honneurs mensongers;
Faites la despartir de ces tons estrangers,
A fin qu'à ce beau mont plus sage elle s'amuse.

Tymanthes malheureux, dont le pinceau s'abuse
A peindre d'Amatonte, & d'Adon les vergers,
Quittez ces Meurtes feints, & ces feints Orangers,
Peignez ces Oliuiers la gloire de Iebuse.

Chantons, peignons ensemble en ces Christiques vers
Ces arbres tousiours beaux, tousiours vifs, tousiours verts,
Et le mystere grand dont l'amour me transporte.

Redisons aux croyans, que ce parfait amant
Parmy les oliuiers commence son torment,
Pour nous marquer la grace, & la paix qu'il aporte.

[21]

Quand Rachel s'accoucha (pour son dernier mal-heur)
Du petit Beniamin, les tranchées roulantes
Par son ventre affligé, furent si violentes
Qu'elle perdit en fin l'auiuante chaleur.

Sur le point que la mort abbatoit sa valeur,
Qu'elle sentit en fin ses forces s'écoulantes,
Mourant elle forma ces paroles dolentes,
Ce fils sera nommé le fils de ma douleur.

Christ ainsi sur le point d'enfanter son Eglise
En mourant sur la Croix, ià desia la baptise
Par ce propos qu'il dit à ce premier effort.

Puis donc que de sa mort elle prendra naissance,
Ne luy doit-elle pas cette recognoissance,
De se dire à tousiours la fille de sa mort?

[6]

Profane Amphions who employ the Muse
To honour but the lies of Helicon
Bid her abandon now that foreign tone
To play on this fair mount and grow more wise.

Wretched Timanthes all, whose brush for shame
Paints Cyprian bowers of Aphrodite's loves
Leave those false myrtles, faithless orange groves:
Paint these true olives of Jerusalem.

Come, let us sing, depict in Christly strain
These trees for ever fair, alive and green
And the great mystery whose love has wings:

Remind believers that this perfect Lover
Among the olive-trees begins to suffer
As earnest of the grace and peace he brings.

[21]

When Rachel was in labour (her last grief)
With little Benjamin, the cramps that rolled
Across her stricken belly left her cold
Despairing from their violence for her life.

When she found there was no more time to borrow
And felt her strength slipping at length away
These were the woeful words she tried to say:
'This son is to be called Son of my Sorrow.'

'Sorrowful unto death': when he said this
Before he died for her upon the Cross
Christ named his Church before he gave her birth.

So since she will be born because he died
Does she not evermore owe gratitude
Calling herself the daughter of his death?

[29]

L'humblesse est le rayon qui perce le nuage,
Qui porte au ciel les vœus d'vn cœur deuotieux.
Le souuerain Seigneur voit d'vn œil gratieux
La priere de l'humble, & sa peine soulage.

JESVS, (de qui la vie est nostre apprentissage)
Ne se parque en priant d'vn maintien glorieux,
N'esleue vers le ciel vn front audacieux,
Ains à genoux prosterne en terre son visage.

C'il qui voit dans la prée, au plus sec des chaleurs,
L'eau clere qui surgeonne emmy l'herbe, & les fleurs,
N'en peut, sans se baisser, contenter son enuie.

Bele & viue fontaine, on ne peut boire aussi
De vostre eau, iaillissante à l'eternele vie,
Sans qu'on se mette bas, & se prosterne ainsi.

[38]

S'escartant donc vn peu de sa maiestueuse
Et diuine grandeur, pour à nous s'attacher,
Il permet aux douleurs de si prés l'approcher
Qu'il en sue le sang: ô sueur fructueuse!

Le raisin ne rend point sa liqueur gracieuse
Sans premier qu'on le presse: ô sacre-sainte Chair,
Le pressoir de la Croix n'ose encor' vous toucher,
Et desia vous rendez cette humeur precieuse.

O mon ame, contemple icy ton Redempteur,
Seul, de nuict, tout couuert d'vne rouge moiteur,
Ou plustost de pur sang: voy combien il endure.

Veille donc, prie donc, & te range à son flanc,
Pour toy ce dur combat doit vuider en peu d'heure
Ses arteres d'esprits, & ses veines de sang.

[29]

Humility is the cloud-piercing ray
Which lifts the prayers of pious hearts on high:
The sovereign Lord sees with a gracious eye
The humble man's prayer, soothes his woes away.

Jesus, to whose life we are articled
Puts on no grandiose bearing when he prays
Nor does he bare to heaven a shameless gaze
But kneels and bows his face towards the mould.

He who sees in the meadow as noon towers
Clear water bubbling in the grass and flowers
Cannot, unless he stoop, fulfil his wishes:

Fair, living fountain, neither can we drink
Your water which to life eternal gushes
Unless we stoop, and down on our knees sink.

[38]

Moving aside a little from his great
Majestic godhead, to be near to us
He allows sorrows to come in so close
That he sweats blood from them: O fruitful sweat!

The grape does not give up its gracious juice
Without first being pressed: O sacred flesh
The Cross's winepress dares not yet to crush
Now you give off this moisture of great price!

My soul, make your Redeemer here your study
Alone, at night, a red dew on his body
That is, pure blood: see how he bears the strain.

Watch then and pray, be numbered at his side:
For your sake this harsh battle soon will drain
His arteries of spirit, his veins of blood.

[48]

Son front majestueux, sa graue Royauté,
Ses yeux estincelans, son pouuoir redoutable,
Son dernier iugement (à tous espouuantable)
Ne peuuent rien Iudas, sur ta desloyauté.

Ses propos doux-coulans, sa douce priuauté,
Ta charge en sa maison, la faueur de sa table,
Cet accueil (qui rendroit vn barbare traittable)
Ne sçauroient adoucir ta fiere cruauté.

Ainsi du beau Soleil la torche matiniere
Fait musser les Hibous dans leur noire taniere:
Car la clarté brillante est haineuse à leurs yeux.

De mesme pour neant sur le sablon distille
La fecondante humeur, qui découle des Cieux,
Plus il est arrousé, plus il est infertille.

[79]

Des peureux oiselets la troupe gazoüillarde
Au simple mouuement, au moindre petit bruit,
D'vn caillou, qu'vn passant dans le taillis hazarde
Part, s'enuole en desordre, & s'escarte, & s'enfuit.

Cependant qu'ils s'en vont où la peur les conduit,
Ils trouuent le peril de leur fuite coüarde,
L'vn donne dans la glu qui sa fuite retarde,
L'autre dans le filet qu'on a tendu la nuict.

Christ ainsi prisonnier fut la pierre iettée
Au milieu de sa troupe aussi tost escartée,
Chacun des siens se lasche à sa fragilité.

Et fuyant leur salut, pour fuïr la potence,
L'vn donne variable au ret de l'inconstance,
L'autre se iette au glu de l'infidelité.

[48]

His kingly brow, his solemn royalty
His twinkling eyes, his formidable power
And his last judgement which all men must fear
Have nothing, Judas, on your treachery.

His gentle talk, his sweet intimacy
Your task, your place at table in his household
This welcome which would make a savage mild
Could never soften your proud cruelty.

Just as the fair torch of the morning sun
Drives owls away to lurk in their dark den
Because bright light is hateful to their eyes

Likewise for nothing on the bare terrain
The fruitful moisture drips down from the skies:
The more watered it is, the more barren.

[79]

The timid little birds' twittering tribe
At the mere motion, at the slightest noise
A pebble makes when tossed into the scrub
Goes, flies off in confusion, scatters, flees.

Yet while their terror regulates their flight
They meet the peril of their cowardice:
One ends up in the lime that slows its pace
Another in the net spread out last night.

Christ taken prisoner is thus the stone
No sooner in the midst of his tribe thrown
But scattering them, whose frailty turns them loose:

Fleeing salvation that they may flee butchery
One ends up fluttering in the net of treachery
Another in the lime of faithlessness.

[88]

Maintefois i'ay tenté de vous suiure, ô ma vie,
Par les sentiers cognus que vous m'auez ouuerts:
Mais tousiours, mais tousiours, vos ennemis diuers
M'empoignant au linceul m'ont la force rauie.

Ores que sainctement vostre Esprit me conuie,
De retracer vos pas, par les pas de ces vers,
Ce monde, ce charmeur, cet ennemy peruers,
Me prenant au manteau veut frustrer mon enuie.

De mile vains objets il rend mon cœur épris
D'ont l'amour me tient tant, & si longuement pris,
Qu'à peine auray-je temps de vous suiure au Caluaire.

Faites donc (s'il vous plait) ô Seigneur desormais
Que de l'Adolescent imitant l'exemplaire
Ie quitte ces habits au monde pour iamais.

[91]

Or sus donc serrez fort, liez fort, ô canaille
Celuy qui vient à vous pour dénoüer vos nœuds,
Tiraillez, trauaillez cestui-cy qui trauaille,
Pour soulager les griefs de vos trauaux peineux.

Resserrez, captiuez dans vn roc cauerneux
Cil, qui sa liberté pour vos libertez baille:
Combatez abatez cétui-cy qui bataille
Pour abatre (abatu) vos antiques haineux.

O liens, ô trauaux, ô mystiques estreintes,
O combats, si les Juifs de vos fortes espreintes
Ne font bien leur profit, profitez les sur nous.

Déliez nos liens, soulagez nos miseres,
Deliurez nous des fers de l'eternel courroux,
Et combatez l'effort de nos forts aduersaires.

[88]

Often have I tried to follow you, my life
Along familiar paths your mercy shows
But always, but always your several foes
Have seized me by the sheet, my strength borne off.

Now that I hear your Spirit's holy call
To mark your footsteps with these measured feet
This world, this charmer, this foe is a cheat
Clutching me by the cloak, thwarting my will.

By a thousand vanities I am possessed,
So much, so long besotted, I am pressed
For time to follow you to Calvary:

Henceforth, Lord, grant that learning by your favour
From the young man who slipped his captors, I
May leave these habits to the world for ever.

[91]

So up now, tightly grasp and bind, you rabble
One who comes to unbind your every bond
Torment and trouble one who takes the trouble
To soothe the troubles of your deep despond.

Confine, hold captive in a rocky cavern
One who, to be made free with, offers bail
Beat, beat down one who, beaten, will not fail
To beat down those who long with you have striven.

O bonds, O torments, mystical constraints,
Struggles, if to the Jews your pain presents
No profit, then grant us a dividend:

Unbind your bonds and soothe our many woes
Free us from wrathful fetters at life's end
And beat the might of all our mighty foes!

[96]

Magnanime Samson, Nazarien Alcide,
Souffrez-vous ces liens, ces fers iniurieux?
Où sont de vos cheueux les faits victorieux?
Las vous voila trahi par ce faux parricide.

Miserables fuitifs qui pollus d'homicide
Exilez, habitez ces lieux mysterieux,
Vous voila dés demain libres, & glorieux
Le grand Prestre mourra par l'effort Jsacide.

On l'a pris, on le tient, on le mene en prison.
Dés que Phœbus aura remonté l'horizon
On fera de son Corps vn sanglant sacrifice.

O Iuifs que pensez vous de sa mort rapporter?
Vous verrez de Gazam les portes emporter,
Jl destruira mourant vous, & vostre Edifice.

[99]

Iardin infortuné que le mal-heur rauage
Prenez, prenez le dueil, vostre bon Iardinier
Ne vous reuerra plus, on la fait prisonnier
Vous voila desormais vn noir desert sauuage.

Ha que vous souffrirez de maux en ce vefuage
Ce feconde Soleil, cet Aspect matinier
Qui faisoit refleurir vostre esmail printanier,
Est ores esclipsé par vn espais nuage.

Que toute vostre humeur s'escoule ores en pleur
Puis qu'on vous a raui vostre plus belle fleur,
Puis qu'on vous a priué de vostre alme Rosée.

Sortant du vieil Edem, il fut au moins permis
Au premier Iardinier d'auoir son Espousée:
Le second n'est suiui que de ses ennemis.

[96]

Brave Samson, Hercules of Nazareth
What bonds, what shameful shackles do you bear?
Where are the mighty exploits of your hair?
You fall to sacrilege and broken faith.

O wretched fugitives who, stained with blood
Live out your exile in those secret places
Tomorrow you will be free to show your faces
When the high Priest by Israel's hand has died.

He is arrested, held, taken to prison:
As soon as Phoebus tinges the horizon
His body will be made a red example.

O Jews, what do you think to gain that day?
You will see the doors of Gaza borne away.
By dying he will destroy you and your Temple.

[99]

O hapless garden ravaged by distress
Dress, dress in mourning: your good Gardener
No more will see you, he is a prisoner
And you henceforth are a black wilderness.

How you will suffer in this widowhood!
That teeming Sun who smiled on you each morning
And fashioned the spring's jewels for your adorning
Is overshadowed now by a dense cloud.

Let all your moisture waste away in tears
For they have snatched the fairest of your flowers
Stolen the Dew that freshened you to life.

The first gardener was at least allowed
As he left Eden, comfort from his wife:
The second only by his foes is followed.

Premiere Partie
Second Liure

First Part
Second Book

[41]

Harpye au ventre-creux, monstre fecond d'erreur,
Semence de tous maux, Auarice execrable,
L'ame qui te reçoit ne conçoit que fureur,
N'enfante qu'iniustice, & perit miserable.

Pour cette verité cet acte est memorable
Cet auare Iudas n'est pour tout acquereur
Que d'vn rude licol, dont le nœud deplorable
Le garrotte au posteau de l'eternele horreur.

Vous qui béez apres l'auide friandise
De l'or, voyez le fruict de vostre marchandise
Qui perd en se perdant, le Corps, l'Ame, & l'honneur.

De la Lote du gain Sathan vous affriande,
Mais il vous sert en fin l'absynthe empoisonneur
De l'amer desespoir pour derniere viande.

[44]

Les Prestres cependant qui veulent faire croire
Au Romain qu'ils sont tous bien fort religieux
De peur d'estre soüillez n'entrent point au Pretoire,
Pour manger impollus l'Agneau mysterieux.

O Sepulchres blanchis, ô cœurs malicieux.
Ceux qui ne font point cas d'vn crime tout notoire,
A qui l'assasinat n'est pas contagieux,
Craignent qu'vn toict gentil rende leur ame noire?

Ha! que ce bel habit, que ce titre affeté
De la Religion couure d'impieté.
Mais l'imposture en fin son mensonge desserre.

L'hypocrite ressemble à l'Austruche Afriquain,
Contre-faisant l'oyseau, qui d'vn pennage vain
Fait semblant de voler, & ne bouge de terre.

[41]

O hollow-bellied harpy, monster huge
With wrong, seed of all evils, loathsome Greed
The soul receiving you conceives but rage
Brings forth unrighteousness and dies in need.

This deed speaks truth never to be forgot:
This Judas for his pains gains nothing dearer
Than a harsh halter whose unlovely knot
Tethers him fast to everlasting horror.

All you who at the blandishments of gold
Gape greedily, see what your dealings yield
That, spilled, spills body, soul and self-respect:

Satan's lotus entices you, to feed
You on the drug despair and hold you hooked
On bitter wormwood for your final meed.

[44]

Meanwhile the priests, who want to prove to Rome
How deeply they are religious one and all
For fear of taint before the Paschal lamb
Is eaten, stay outside the judgement hall.

O whited sepulchres, hearts full of filth
Who at sheer villainy do not bat an eyelid
These for whom murder brings no risk to health
Fear by a gentile roof to be defilèd!

Ha! How these grand robes, how these fancy titles
Cover Religion's maggot in the vitals:
But falsehood blows its cover in the end.

The hypocrite is like the ostrich, sham
Bird of the south that waving a vain plume
Pretends to fly, and never leaves the ground.

[54]

Blanc est le vestement du grand Pere sans âge
Blancs sont les courtisans de sa blanche maison,
Blanc est de son esprit l'étincelant pennage:
Blanche est de son Agneau la brillante toison.

Blanc est le crespe sainct dont (pour son cher blason)
Aux Nopces de l'Agneau l'Espouse s'aduantage.
Blanc est or' le manteau dont par mesme raison
Cet innocent Espous se pare en son Nopçage.

Blanc estoit l'ornement dont le Pontife vieux
S'affeubloit pour deuot offrir ses vœus aux Cieux:
Blanc est le parement de ce nouueau grand Prestre.

Blanche est la robbe deüe au fort victorieux.
Ce vainqueur (bien qu'il aille à la mort se souzmettre)
Blanc, sur la dure mort triomphe glorieux.

[63]

Aux Monarques vaincueurs la rouge cotte-d'armes
Appartient iustement. Ce Roy victorieux
Est iustement vestu par ces mocqueurs gens-d'armes
D'vn manteau, qui le marque & Prince, & glorieux.

O pourpre emplis mon test de ton ius precieux
Et luy fay distiller mille pourprines larmes,
A tant que meditant ton sens mysterieux,
Du sang trait de mes yeux i'ensanglante ces Carmes.

Ta sanglante couleur figure nos pechez
Au dos de cet Agneau par le Pere attachez:
Et ce Christ t'endossant se charge de nos crimes.

O Christ, ô sainct Agneau, daigne toy de cacher
Tous mes rouges pechez (brindelles des abysmes)
Dans les sanglans replis du manteau de ta chair.

[54]

White is the raiment of the ageless Father
White are the courtiers of his white abode
White is his Spirit's every sparkling feather
White is the bright fleece of the Lamb of God.

White is the holy gauze, her precious blazon
In which the Bride is wedded to the Lamb
White is the mantle which for the same reason
Adorns today the Bridegroom without blame.

White were the holy garments all of linen
In which the pontiff prayed in the beginning:
White the adornment of this new high priest.

White the robe due to one victorious:
This strong one, though death is his only feast
White over harsh death triumphs glorious.

[63]

To conquering monarchs the red coat of arms
Justly belongs. This King, victorious
Is justly clothed by mocking men-at-arms
In robes that dub him prince and glorious.

O purple, fill my head with your dear juice
And make it drip a thousand crimson tears
That as I think on your mysterious
Meaning my eyes' drawn blood may stain these airs.

Your bloody colour figures forth our sin
Bound by the Father to this Lamb's fair skin
And this Christ wearing you bears all our ill.

O Christ, O holy Lamb, I beg you, hold
All my red sins, these kindling-twigs of hell
Hid in your flesh's robe's each bloody fold.

[64]

O Pere dont iadis les mains industrieuses
Cette vigne ont planté, voy comme au lieu du fruict
Qu'elle deut rapporter, ingrate elle produit
Pour couronner ton fils des ronces épineuses.

Ces Epines estoient les peines crimineuses
Des reuoltes de l'homme au Paradis seduit:
Et ce Christ qui sa coulpe, & ses peines détruict
Ces épines arrose, & les rend fructueuses.

Pour deliurer Juda le Pere descendant
D'épines entouré dans vn halier ardant
Fit l'effort merueilleux de sa forte puissance.

Et le Fils descendant du seiour paternel,
Bruslant dans cet halier d'vn amour eternel,
Fait l'épineux effort de nostre deliurance.

[65]

Nature n'a rien fait qu'on doiue mépriser
Sa moindre-petite œuure est encor' fructueuse
Elle a mis au Roseau la vertu merueilleuse
De pouuoir des Serpens les testes écrazer.

Mocqueurs, ce vieux Serpent qui vous a fait ozer
Moquer de ce grand Roy la dextre glorieuse,
Par ce vile Roseau, vous faict prophetizer
Qu'il en écrazera sa teste sourcilleuse.

Mais, ô Christ, ce Roseau que tu prens en tá main,
N'est-il pas bien encor le Symbole germain
De ce vile Gentil que ton Royaume embrasse?

Suis-ie pas ce Roseau, qui te couste si cher,
Qu'or' l'vn, or' l'autre vent de ce monde terrasse,
Si tant soit peu ta main se lasche à me lascher?

[64]

O Father whose hard-working hands of old
Planted this vine, see what it bears instead
Of its own fruit: now to crown your Son's head
A thorny bramble is its thankless yield!

Those thorns were once the punishment to suit
The crime in paradise of man who strayed:
His fault, his punishment are now destroyed
By Christ who waters these thorns, makes them fruit.

For Judah's sake the Father once descended
Into a burning bush with thorns surrounded
And worked the wonders of his mighty power:

The Son descends now from the realms above
Burning in this bush with eternal love
And works salvation at this thorny hour.

[65]

Let none despise whatever nature made.
Her meanest little work is fruitful still:
She has planted in the reed the wondrous skill
The virtuous power to crush the serpent's head.

Mockers, that serpent which once made you dare
To mock this great King's glorious right hand
Thanks to this humble reed makes you declare
That its disdainful head shall soon be ground.

But, Christ, is not this reed which you have gripped
Much more than that the emblem, humbly apt
Of this gentile within your kingdom furled?

For am I not this reed which costs you so
Flattened by every wild wind of this world
If you, however slightly, let me go?

[67]

O Royauté tragique! ô vestement infame!
O poignant Diademe! ô Sceptre rigoureux!
O belle, & chere teste! ô l'amour de mon ame!
O mon Christ seul fidele, & parfait amoureux.

On vous frappe, ô sainct chef, & ces coups douleureux
Font que vostre Couronne en cent lieux vous r'entame
Bourreaux assenez-le d'vne tranchante lame,
Et versez tout à coup ce pourpre genereux.

Faut-il pour vne mort qu'il en souffre dix mille?
He! voyez que le sang, qui de son chef distille
Ses pruneles détrempe, & rend leur iour affreux.

Ce pur sang, ce Nectar, prophané se mélange
A vos sales crachats, dont la sanglante fange
Change ce beau visage en celuy d'vn lepreux.

[68]

Mais que dis-ie, ô mon Prince, ignorant ie diffame
Vos ornemens Royaux? vostre cœur genereux,
Et mon propre interest ne souffrent que ie blâme
Ceux qui vous font pour moy tous ces maux rigoureux.

Ces coups vous sont, mon Christ, plus doux que douleureux
Puis qu'ils font distiller de vostre chef ce Bâme,
Qui (pour cicatrizer les playes de mon Ame)
Seruira desormais d'appareil amoureux.

Ces crachats teints au sang, qui sur vos yeux distille
Les couurent de bourbier: ce bourbier est vtille
A mes yeux, que l'horreur des pechez rend affreux.

La saliue, & la terre, (ô Symbolique fange)
Ont bien guery l'Aueugle: & ce nouueau mélange
De sang, & de crachats guerira ce lepreux.

[67]

O tragic kingship, raiment made most vile
Sharp diadem, O sceptre that brings hurt
O fair, dear head, O lover of my soul
O Christ whose one true Passion pays me court!

They strike you, holy brow, tear you apart
Crown you and from a hundred holes you spill:
Torturers, use a slashing blade and deal
Death with a purple flush from this great heart!

But must he bear ten thousand for one death?
See how the blood drips from his brow beneath
And hideously soaks each once bright eye

Mixing this outraged nectar, this pure blood
With your foul spittle into bloodstained mud
Giving this fair face marks of leprosy!

[68]

But what, Prince, do I say who so revile
Crassly your royal trappings? Your great heart
And my own interest will not have me growl
At those who on my own behalf bring hurt.

These blows, my Christ, perform the sweeter part
Of pain, since from your brow they now distil
This balm to heal the festers of my soul
And henceforth will adorn you paying court.

This spittle streaked with blood that drips beneath
Into your eyes, forms mud: this is a bath
To cleanse the sinful horrors from my eye.

Saliva mixed with earth (symbolic mud!)
Healed the blind man: now spittle mixed with blood
Anew, will heal me of my leprosy.

[69]

Quand ces prophanes mains du deuoir foruoyantes
Eurent sur l'innocent faict leur dernier effort,
Pilate (commandant qu'on l'amenat) r'essort
Vers les Juifs, pour saouler leur rages abboyantes.

VOICY-L'HOMME (dit-il) vos armes flamboyantes
N'ont point sur luy de prise, il n'est digne de mort.
Vueillez donc (à ces mots le bruit fut si tres-fort
Que sa voix se perdit dans ces troupes bruyantes.)

Lors IESVS en manteau fut au peuple monstré,
Couronné de haliers, d'vn vieux Roseau sceptré.
Quel prodige, ô grand Dieu, fais-tu voir sur la terre?

L'Eternele Beauté, la Maiesté des Cieux,
Qui les Anges mutins d'vn seul clin d'œil atterre
Sert ores de ioüet, & de proye aux Hebrieux.

[70]

VOICY-L'HOMME, ô mes yeux, quel obiect deplorable
La honte, le veiller, la faute d'aliment,
Les douleurs, & le sang perdu si largement
L'ont bien tant déformé qu'il n'est plus desirable.

Ces cheueux (l'ornement de son chef venerable)
Sanglantez, herissez, par ce couronnement,
Embroüillez dans ces ioncs, seruent indignement
A son test vlceré d'vne haye execrable.

Ces yeux (tantost si beaux) rébatus, r'enfoncez,
Ressalis, sont helas! deux Soleils éclipsez,
Le coral de sa bouche est ores iaune-pasle.

Les roses, & les lys de son teint sont flétris:
Le reste de son Corps est de couleur d'Opale,
Tant de la teste aux pieds ses membres sont meurtris.

[69]

When these profane hands from their duty straying
Had worked their worst upon the innocent
Pilate commanded he be brought and went
Out to the Jews again to calm their baying.

'Behold the man,' he said: 'your flashing swords
Cannot hold him, he has no right to die.
Therefore be . . .' At these words rose such a cry
From the crazed pack that it drowned out his words.

Then to the people Jesus was displayed
His crown a bush, his sceptre an old reed.
Great God, what is this marvel you reveal?

Eternal beauty, heaven's majesty
Who with a wink hurled Satan's crew to hell
Now serves the Hebrews for a toy, a prey.

[70]

Behold the man – my eyes, the piteous sight:
Dishonour and the lack of sleep, of food
And the pain and the loss of so much blood
Have made him little object of delight.

This hair that decks his holy brow is red
And horrid with the crown they set on him
Entangled in these rushes to its shame
Like a vile hedgerow on his cankered head.

These eyes, so fair once, stricken, sunken, soiled
Alas! are now two suns whose light has failed.
The coral of his mouth is bleached and wan.

Upon his cheeks the rose and lily rot.
Elsewhere his body has turned opaline
So battered are his limbs from head to foot.

[71]

Iadis ce grand Ouurier forma ce grand ouurage
Du petit vniuers, sur son image sainct.
L'œuure de son ouurier les sainctes loix enfreint:
Soudain il se corromp & change de visage.

Cet Ouurier (que l'amour à la Clemence engage)
A pitié de son œuure, il l'excuse, il le plainct:
Et pour le reformer son amour le contrainct
De se raualer tant que d'en prendre l'image.

C'est cet image hideux de nostre genre humain
Qu'en ces mots, VOICY-L'HOMME, exhibe le Romain:
Dieu se cachant de luy sous l'écorce mortele.

Comme autres fois Rachel pour ses derniers adieux
Par les mois de son Sexe (ô pieuse cautele)
Trompa son vieux bon-homme, & luy cacha ses Dieux.

[72]

Le bon vieillard maudit sa primo geniture,
Son mignon, son Ruben pour auoir eshonté
Sur le lict concubin de son Pere monté,
Et paillard violé les loix de la nature.

Et tu souffres, grand Dieu, qu'ores ta nourriture
Ton Hebrieu, ton aisné méprise ta bonté,
Se iette sur ta couche, où ce bouc effronté
A villain deformé ta belle architecture.

Qu'est-ce autre chose, ô Christ, ta saincte humanité
Que l'Espouse, & le lict de ta Diuinité?
Ce puant la poluë, & d'opprobres couuerte.

Et maintenant ce Cham découure à ses Germains
La honte paternele, & rit à gueule ouuerte
O Dieu, que ne sent il tes vengeresses mains?

[71]

Once this great Workman fashioned this great work –
The microcosm, which his likeness shows.
But the work breaks his Workman's holy laws:
His face bears suddenly corruption's mark.

This Workman, bound by love to pity weakness
Has mercy on his work, grieves, and forgives him:
To fashion him anew his great love drives him
To lower himself till he takes on his likeness.

This is the hideous likeness of the human
In this *Behold the man* shown by the Roman:
God hiding from him under mortal shell

As in the old days Rachel leaving home
By pleading woman's flowers (O pious guile)
Tricked her old man and hid his gods from him.

[72]

The old man laid a curse on his firstborn
His darling Reuben who had boldly strayed
Upon the bed of his good father's maid
And lewdly laughed all nature's laws to scorn.

You suffer, great God, that your elder son
The Jew you cared for, sets your gifts at naught
Leaps on your litter, where this shameless goat
Has wickedly deformed your fair design.

O Christ, what is your white humanity
But bride and bed of your divinity?
This foul one soils it, smears it with disgrace.

And now this Ham uncovers to his kind
His father's nakedness, laughs in his face.
God, why does he not feel your vengeful hand?

[73]

Sionides sortez, venez voir l'equipage
Du grand Roy Salomon: le voicy couronné
D'vn nouueau Diademe, au iour de son Nopçage,
Qui luy fut par sa mere en partage donné.

Ce plus que Salomon d'opprobres foisonné
Sort couronné de ioncs (creus dans le Marescage
De vostre Synagogue) à ce iour ordonné
Pour consommer çà bas son heureux Mariage.

A ce iour par sa mort, ô Nopçage immortel,
Son Eglise il épouse, & la fiere Bethel
(Sa Mere sous la loy) d'épines le couronne.

O belle, & chere Epouse, ô parfaicte amitié,
C'est pour vous qu'il s'expose à la rage felonne
De celle, qui n'a point d'amour, ny de pitié.

[85]

Pontifes possedez d'vne fureur extreme,
Cet adueu conuaincra vostre temerité,
Cesar est vostre Roy, donc la posterité
Du benit de Iacob n'a plus de Diademe.

Or si Iuda ne peut par vostre Oracle mesme
Estre iamais priué du Sceptre merité,
Que l'Enuoyé ne vienne, il est donc verité
Que Christ est l'Enuoyé du Monarque supreme.

Ha! pauurets, il est vray, le Messie est venu,
Et Iuda pour auoir son vray Roy mécognu
S'alliant au Gentil perd ores sa Couronne.

A vos traistres Ayeuls aduint vn tel méchef,
S'escrians en Pharan d'vne rage felonne
Retournons en Egypte, & nous creons vn chef.

[73]

Daughters of Zion, go forth, see the array
Of great King Solomon: behold him crowned
With a new diadem on his wedding day
Which is his portion from his mother's hand.

This more than Solomon with shame festooned
Comes crowned with rushes (they grew in the mire
Of your own synagogue) this day ordained
To consummate his happy marriage there.

This day by dying he will wed his Bride
The Church (immortal wedding!) and the pride
Of those the Law calls kin crown him with thorn.

O fair, dear Bride, O happiest conjunction
For you he faces the vile rage and scorn
Of those who have no love and no compunction.

·

[85]

'No king but Caesar': so, chief priests, you roar
And now the case against you can proceed.
Since Caesar is your king, the blessed seed
Of Jacob has a diadem no more.

If Judah can by your own oracle
Never give up the sceptre once deserved
Until the Envoy come, then it is proved
Christ is the Envoy from the Lord of all.

Ah! poor things, it is true, Messiah has come
And Judah who has not acknowledged him
Joined to the gentile, loses now his crown.

At such a point your treacherous fathers tripped
Crying for evil rage in wild Paran:
'Let us make a captain, and return to Egypt.'

Premiere Partie
Troisieme Liure

First Part
Third Book

[10]

Debout, parmi l'horreur des charognes relantes
En cette orde voirie, il voit de tous costez
De ses durs ennemis les troupes insolentes,
Et de sa dure mort les outils apprestez.

Puis, las! si tant soit peu ses yeux sont arrestez
Sur les yeux maternels, leurs pruneles parlantes,
S'entredisant Adieu, vont perdant leurs clartez
Par l'effort redoublé des larmes ruisselantes.

Tandis on le despouille à fin de le coucher
Sur la Croix, mais helas! c'est tout vif l'escorcher:
Car le sang a colé sa tunique à ses playes.

Ces tormens sont cruels: Mais beaucoup plus l'affront.
Voicy, mon Redempteur, vos paroles bien vrayes
Que la honte, & l'opprobre ont couuert vostre front.

[14]

Les bourreaux donc pressez par les voix gromelantes
Des parricides Iuifs forcenans de courroux,
Portent sur cet Aigneau leurs griffes violantes;
Le iettent sur la Croix pour y marquer les trous.

Jl se releue vn peu sur ses foibles genoux,
Offre au Pere Eternel ses prieres bruslantes
D'amour, puis se recouche, & ses playes coulantes
Marquent au bois les lieux, pour y ficher les clous.

A peine le pauuret acheua de s'estendre
Sur la Croix, que luy mesme encommença de tendre
Sa main gauche premiere à la mercy du fer.

La gauche auec le cœur a plus de voisinage:
Pource il veut que premiere on l'ouure en témoignage
Qu'il leur ouure son cœur pour nous fermer l'Enfer.

[10]

Amid the horror of stale meat he stands
In this foul shambles, seeing all about
His harsh foes ready in their shameless bands
Their tools with which his life will be put out.

However fleetingly he rests his gaze
Upon his Mother, each bright pupil blurs
In the exchange of silent last goodbyes
With the redoubled force of streaming tears.

To lay him on the Cross they now remove
His robe, and they are flaying him alive
Because the blood has stuck it to his sores.

Cruel, these tortures: still more the disgrace.
Hear, my Redeemer, what your psalm declares:
'I have borne reproach, shame hath covered my face'.

[14]

The torturers whom the sacrilegious Jews
Urge on with mutterings and maddened howls
Lay now upon the Lamb their violent claws
Throw him down on the Cross to mark the holes.

He staggers to his knees which soon will fail him
Offers the eternal Father scalding prayers
Of love, sinks back, and his discharging sores
Mark out upon the wood where they will nail him.

Hardly has he, the poor dear, done with stretching
Out on the Cross when he himself is reaching
His left hand first to iron's untender will.

The left is nearer to the heart: we see
By wanting this one opened first that he
Opens his heart to them, to us shuts hell.

[15]

Soudain que sur le trou cette main fut tenduë,
Dans sa paume on enfonce à grans coups de marteau
Vn clou gros & quarré, iusqu'au dos du posteau:
Sans qu'on ait de sa bouche vne plainte entenduë.

Mais la forge du fer vous estoit defenduë
O Juifs vous n'auiez point ni coutre, ni rasteau,
Ni coignée, ni cloux, ni maillet, ni cousteau
Qui vous a d'en auoir la liberté renduë?

Le fer n'osoit toucher aux pierres de l'Autel,
Le fer n'entra iamais au Temple de Bethel,
Et le fer au vray Temple au iourd'huy fait outrage.

Maudites soient Tubal, tes forgeronnes mains:
Mais benites plustost, puis qu'ores leur ouurage
Sert d'instrument vtile au salut des humains.

[16]

On vient à la main droite; elle a eu bel à teindre
De sang le lieu du trou: il est plus loing pourtant
Puis les nerfs retirez ont retiré d'autant,
Et racourci le bras, elle n'y peut atteindre.

Aussi tost d'vne corde on commence à l'estreindre
Puis à force on la tire, & la retire tant
Qu'on la fait ioindre au trou, où le bourreau plantant
L'autre clou, fut pourpré du sang qu'il fit épreindre.

De mesme au trou d'embas, les pieds demeurent cours,
Les bourreaux ont de mesme à la corde recours,
C'est lors qu'on oit crouler cette belle structure.

Tout ce corps se desjoint, & le dur craquement
Des membres disloquez, & des nerfs la rupture,
Font croire qu'on veut faire vn vif demembrement.

[15]

Immediately this hand is stretched out, hard
Into the palm with juddering blows they whack
A fat square nail that goes straight through the stake:
Yet not a murmur from his lips is heard.

But forging was forbidden you, O Jews:
You had no coulter, no axe and no rake
And mallets, nails and knives you must not make
So who has given you these tools to use?

The iron that dared not touch the altar stones
Nor see the temple that was Solomon's
Today on the true Temple commits rape.

Accursed, O Tubal, be your blacksmith's hand:
But blessed rather, since what it could shape
Is now the instrument that saves mankind.

[16]

They come to the right hand: it fails to touch
With blood the hole's place. There is far to go:
The shrunken sinews have so shrunk and so
Shortened the arm that now it cannot reach.

They start forthwith to stretch it with a rope
Tugging and tugging this until the hole
Is met, when driving in the other nail
The torturer stains himself as blood spurts up.

Similarly below, the feet come short:
The torturers to the rope again resort.
Then we can hear this handsome frame collapse:

The sagging body and the brittle crack
As limb is dislocated, sinew snaps
Are like a man being torn upon the rack.

First Part, Third Book   51

[18]

Ses pieds sont donq percez (comme il auoit predit)
Percée est sa main gauche: & sa droite est percée:
Sa peau, par trop tenduë, est par tout creuacée:
Et ses os sont comptez par ce peuple maudit.

Or nos durs Circoncis craignans qu'il ne rendit
L'esprit auparauant que la Croix fut dressée
S'escrient qu'on l'esleue: & la troupe amassée
Des sergens, des bourreaux à cela se roidit.

Ces impiteux ouuriers, dépitez qu'on les tance,
Attrainent brusquement cette lourde potence
Pour du creux preparé le bas bout approcher:

Puis la leuant debout, la pointe on precipite
Si roide dans ce trou creuzé sur le rocher
Que le coup s'en va bruire au centre du Cocyte.

[19]

Les sanglotans helas des amis soucieux,
Les murmurantes voix des troupes suruenuës,
Les esclatans abois des Hebrieux factieux,
Les hauts cris des bourreaux montent iusques aux nuës.

Maints auoient iusqu'icy leurs langues contenuës,
Qui rompent le silence: & les deuotieux
Secrets (ne craignez plus les Iuifs malicieux)
Laschent ores la bonde aux larmes retenuës.

He! qui les retiendroit? Au contre-coup mortel
De la cheute du bois, l'esbranlement fut tel,
Qu'il n'a playe en son corps, qui n'en soit reouuerte.

Presque, presque les cloux ont my-party les mains,
La terre d'alentour de son sang est couuerte,
Et son Test se r'attache à ces joncs inhumains.

[18]

So, as he has foretold, his feet are pierced
And his left hand is pierced, pierced too his right
His skin all cracked from being stretched too tight
His bones are numbered by that people accursed.

Our circumcised now fear he will give up
The ghost before the Cross is brought to stand:
Lift it! they harshly cry, and the whole band
Of sergeants, torturers brace themselves to grip.

These workmen whom no tender cares inhibit
Vexed at the scolding, yank this heavy gibbet
Dragging its base towards the space prepared

Then raising it upright, into the hole
Carved in the rock they ram the point so hard
The impact jars the wailing depths of hell.

[19]

The sobbing cries of sympathetic friends
The muffled voices of the gathering crowds
The yap of Hebrews bent on their own ends
The shouts of torturers rise towards the clouds.

Many who hitherto were reticent
Break silence, and the secret worshippers
For whom the evil Jews hold no more fears
Now to their stoppered sorrows give full vent.

Well, what would stop them? At the fatal shock
As the wood finds the hole, such is the knock
It bursts afresh his body's every wound.

The nails have almost, almost split his hands
His blood is spattered on the earth all round
And on his head the cruel crown rebounds.

[20]

L'amour l'a de l'Olympe icy bas fait descendre:
L'amour l'a fait de l'homme endosser le peché:
L'amour luy a des-ja tout son sang fait espandre:
L'amour l'a fait souffrir qu'on ait sur luy craché:

L'amour a ces haliers à son chef attaché:
L'amour fait que sa Mere à ce bois le void pendre:
L'amour a dans ses mains ces rudes cloux fiché:
L'amour le va tantost dans le sepulchre estendre.

Son amour est si grand, son amour est si fort
Qu'il attaque l'Enfer, qu'il terrasse la mort,
Qu'il arrache à Pluton sa fidele Euridice.

Belle pour qui ce beau meurt en vous bien-aimant
Voyez s'il fut iamais vn si cruel supplice,
Voyez s'il fut iamais vn si parfait Amant.

[21]

Il est donq monté, belle, au gibet ordonné,
Pour vous faire monter à son Throsne supreme,
Jl a son tendre chef de ronces couronné,
Pour ceindre vostre chef d'vn brillant diademe.

Il patit des tormens le torment plus extreme,
Pour satisfaire au mal qu'il vous a pardonné,
Il vuide ores de sang son corps liuide, & bléme,
Pour le prix dont prodigue il vous a rançonné.

Il souffre patient qu'à ce iour on fabrique
Des logettes pour vous dans la pierre mystique
De son corps, & sa voix vous semond d'y venir.

Belle, venez y donq, vostre Espoux le commande:
Et pourtant de bien-faits dont il veut vous benir
Donnez luy vostre cœur, c'est tout ce qu'il demande.

[20]

Love brought him from Olympus here below
Love made him bear upon his back man's sin
Love has already made all his blood flow
Love made him suffer being spat upon.

Love has rammed down upon his brow this bush
Love makes his Mother see him hanged on wood
Love drove into his hands these nails that crush
Love in the tomb will shortly see him laid.

So great his love, his great love is so mighty
That he storms hell, upon death has no pity
Snatches from Pluto his Eurydice:

O fair one whom this Fair One dies to favour
See, did man ever die so cruelly
See, was there ever such a perfect lover.

[21]

So, fair one, he has gone up to the appointed
Gallows, that you may rise and reign supreme
And he has crowned his tender brow with pointed
Thorns, to gird yours with a bright diadem.

Of torture he is bearing the extreme
To expiate your ill he has forgiven:
Of blood he drains his wan and livid frame
To pay your ransom, prodigally given.

Docile this day he suffers them to fashion
Nooks for you in the rockface of his Passion
Which is himself, and summons you to come.

So, fair one, come, for your Bridegroom commands.
So many blessings: to be blessed with them
Give him your heart, that is all he demands.

[22]

Du vray Deucalion le bois industrieux
Qui soustint la fureur du general naufrage,
Dans vne mer de sang à cette heure surnage,
Pour sauuer les humains des bouillons stygieux.

Le vieux Arc bigarré (signe presagieux
De la fin du deluge, & mis en témoignage
Qu'on ne souffriroit plus des ondes le rauage)
Est maintenant courbé sur ce bois precieux.

Puis que ce Nuau peint des couleurs de l'Opale
Calmoit les flots, ce corps rouge, liuide, & pasle
Pourra bien de son Pere appaiser le courroux.

Par ce gage sacré de ta chere alliance
Je t'adiure, ô grand Dieu, qu'ore, & tousiours pour nous
Ton courroux iusticier cede à ta patience.

[23]

L'autel des vieux parfums dans Solyme encensé,
Fait or' d'vne voirie vn Temple venerable,
Où du Verbe incarné l'Hypostase adorable
S'offre tres-odorante à son Pere offensé.

Le vieux Pal, sur lequel jadis fut ageancé
En Edom le Serpent aux mordus secourable,
Esleue ores celuy qui piteux a pensé
Du vieux Serpent d'Edem la morsure incurable.

Le pressoir de la Vigne en Caluaire est dressé,
Où ce fameux raisin ce pressoir a pressé,
Pour noyer dans son vin nos lethales Viperes.

L'eschele Jsraëlite est posée en ce lieu,
Sur laquele auiourd'huy s'appuyant l'homme-Dieu,
Nous fait iouïr des biens qu'il promit à nos Peres.

[22]

The true Deucalion's assiduous wood
Which rode the storm when all the world was wrecked
At this hour on a surge of blood is rocked
To save mankind from where the damned are stewed.

The motley bow of old (a sign that showed
The flood was over, witnessing that we
Should bear no more the onslaught of the sea)
Is lately bowed upon this precious wood.

Since that cloud with the opal's tints suffused
Settled the waves, this body, red, pale, bruised
Will surely still his Father's swelling wrath.

By your dear covenant to which we cling
Great God I beg for us now and henceforth
That your just wrath yield to longsuffering.

[23]

The altar censed in old Jerusalem
Now makes a temple of a slaughterhouse
Where the incarnate Word's hypostasis
Sweetens his Father with his fair perfume.

The pole on which the serpent once was raised
In Edom to relieve the serpent's bite
Now lifts up him who, merciful, has eased
Where Eden's serpent bit, and cured it quite.

On Calvary the winepress is set up
Where this press has pressed out this famous grape
To drown our lethal vipers in its wine.

Jacob's ladder is put up in this place
On which today the propped God-man grants us
Possession where our fathers got a sign.

[24]

Voicy le seur Baston, qui seruit de bateau,
Au bon-homme Iacob dans l'onde Iordanide,
Voicy du fier Geant le Philistin couteau,
Qui enuoya son maistre au manoir Eumenide.

Voicy le fort Trident, qui le flot Neptunide
Mépartant, fit aux Juifs vn chemin seur, & beau:
Et qui le r'assemblant sur l'ost Pharaonide
Fit que toute l'Egypte eut vn mesme tombeau.

Voicy le Bois sucrin dont ce bon Capitaine,
Emmielant le fiel de l'amere fontaine,
Accoisa d'Israël les murmurans abbois.

Mariniers, qui singlez vers la terre promise,
Pour surgir à son port ayez pour entremise
Ce Baston, ce Couteau, ce Trident, & ce Bois.

[25]

O Croix n'aguere infame, horrible, espouuantable,
Ton antique scandale est ores aboly,
Christ a de l'Eternel par son sang ramoly
Le courroux, qui te fit iadis si redoutable.

Ce Nectar, par qui seul le monde est rachetable,
T'arrosant, a changé ton Absynthe, en Moly
Et ton bois raboteux si doucement poly,
Qu'il est or' des esleus le seiour delectable.

Belle Tour de Dauid, forte de deux remparts,
Où pendent mille escus: à toy de toutes parts
Accourent les mortels. He! soy donq ma retraite.

Tu brises auiourd'huy les portes des Enfers,
Fay que ta sainte Image en mon ame pourtraite
Brise ainsi quelque iour, ma prison, & mes fers.

[24]

This is the staff which turned into a boat
For worthy Jacob on the Jordan's wave
This is the giant's sword David drew out
Which from the Fates its master could not save.

This is the trident with which Israel crossed
Neptune's red flood, and a safe passage gave
Drawing the sea back over Pharaoh's host
So that all Egypt sank in the same grave.

This is the wood with which this Admiral
To honey turned the bitter fountain's gall
Quieted the barking Hebrews where they stood:

Sailors who tack towards the promised land
To reach its port, take for your journey's end
This staff, this sword, this trident and this wood.

[25]

O Cross, once shameful, frightful, full of dread
Your ancient scandal now is done away:
Christ with his blood was able to allay
God's wrath with which our direst fears were fed.

The world is ransomed only by this nectar
That, sprinkling you, turns wormwood into moly
And smooths your rough wood till it is so holy
That it is now the place where the elect are.

Fair tower of David with two ramparts strong
Decked with a thousand shields, towards you throng
Mortals from all sides: be then my retreat!

This is the day you smash the gates of hell:
Grant that your sacred mark on my soul set
May some day smash my shackles and my jail.

[26]

Sathan par le bois vert nostre ayeule rauit:
Iesus par le bois sec à Sathan l'a rauie.
Le bois vert à l'Enfer nostre ayeule asseruit:
Le bois sec a d'Enfer la puissance asseruie.

Sathan sur le bois vert vit sa rage assouuie:
Iesus sur le bois sec son amour assouuit.
Le bois vert donna mort à toute ame, qui vit:
Le bois sec (ô merueille!) à tous morts donne vie.

Le bois sec auiourd'huy triomphe du bois vert,
Le vert ferma le Ciel: le sec la reouuert,
Et nous y reconduit par voyes fort aisées.

Jl a tout satisfait: il a tout merité,
Sur ce bois sec la grace atteint la verité:
La iustice, & la paix s'y sont entrebaisées.

[27]

Quand au sortir d'Egypte Jsraël combatoit,
Vers le poisle d'azur son Pasteur venerable
Tendoit ses foibles mains, & ialoux debatoit
Auec Dieu, pour aux siens le rendre secourable.

Tant qu'il les esleuoit sur l'appuy fauorable
De son frere & de Hur, son ost l'autre batoit:
Dés qu'il les mettoit bas (ô mystere admirable)
Amalec Israël à ses pieds abatoit.

Ainsi tant que le Christ eut ses mains abatuës,
Nos ames ont esté rudement combatuës
Par les noirs escadrons de l'Amalec d'embas:

Mais depuis qu'il les a sur la Croix estenduës,
Sous l'appuy de deux cloux, nous gaignons les combas:
Les victoires des siens par tout sont entenduës.

[26]

Satan by green wood our first mother snatched:
Jesus by dry wood Satan's wiles has matched.
Green wood to hell our first mother enslaved.
Dry wood from hell's power all her kin has saved.

Satan on green wood saw his fury sated:
Jesus on dry wood his love consummated.
Green wood brought death to every soul alive:
Dry wood (O wonder!) makes the dead alive.

Dry wood on this day triumphs over green:
Green wood shut heaven, dry wood lets us in
Opening paths to glory with no bother.

He has all expiated, all deserved:
On this dry wood by grace all truth is served
And righteousness and peace have kissed each other.

[27]

When upon leaving Egypt Israel fought,
His saintly shepherd to heaven's canopy
Held out his feeble hands in hot debate
With God, for his help in his people's fray.

As long as they were up, supported by
Aaron and Hur, these had the upper hand:
As soon as they were down (choice mystery!)
Amalek beat Israel into the ground.

Likewise, as long as Jesus' hands were slack
Our souls were harshly beaten by the black
Battalions of the Amalek below:

But since upon the Cross he stretched them out
Supported by two nails, we have won through
And all lands ring with our triumphant shout.

[29]

Iusqu'au Ciel voirement, au comble de l'Empyre
Cet Arbre de la Croix esleue sa hauteur,
Et nul ne peut atteindre au Ciel de son Empire
Que celuy, qui des Cieux est le supreme Autheur.

D'vn rien créer ce Tout, en estre Protecteur,
Animer ce bourbier, qui tantost ne respire
Que le Ciel, & tantost contre le Ciel conspire,
Fut chose bien aisée à nostre Redempteur.

Mais que pour ce bourbier il se soit fait passible,
Qu'il soit pendu pour luy: Non, il n'est pas possible
De l'entendre: ce fait nostre raison destruit.

Bien sçauons nous que c'est dans le centre du monde
Que cet Arbre est planté, pour marque que son fruit
Est pour tous les bourgeois de la machine ronde.

[30]

Cet Arbre est foisonnant en mille fruits diuers,
En amour tres-parfait, en iustice equitable:
Mais la misericorde est la plus delectable,
Dont sans cesse il fournit largement l'vniuers.

Ces beaux fruits sont tousiours d'vn fueillage couuerts,
Qui ne decheoit iamais, c'est la parole stable
De ce Crucifié, dont la foy veritable
Fait renaistre, & nourrit nos espoirs tousiours verts.

Son ombrage amoureux sous lequel on repose,
Est sa grace, qui ferme à toute heure s'oppose
A nos trois ennemis, & nous tient à couuert.

Et les oyseaux nichans en ces rameaux fragiles
Sont nos affections, qui se guindent agiles,
Et se nichent aux trous dont ce corps est ouuert.

[29]

Up to the very sky, the topmost heaven
This tree that is the Cross projects its height
And power to reach its Empire's roof is given
Only to him who made it with his might.

To shape this All from nothing, be its guard
Breathe life into this dust which sometimes plots
A course for heaven, sometimes against heaven plots
Was for our great Redeemer nothing hard.

That for this dust he should be made to suffer
To hang for it – oh no, our thought can offer
No explanation in its vain pursuit.

Full well we know this Tree is planted clean
In the world's centre, showing that its fruit
Is for all commons of the round machine.

[30]

A thousand various fruits regale this Tree:
There is perfect love, fair-minded righteousness
But mercy has the most delicious juice
Which for the universe flows ceaselessly.

These fair fruits are for ever covered up
With leaves that never fall, firm words of truth
Spoken by the one crucified, whose faith
Revives and renders evergreen our hope.

Its loving shade beneath which mankind rests
Is his grace, which at every hour resists
Our three foes, and its charge in shelter keeps

And the birds nesting on each tender bough
Are our affections, which climb nimbly to
Nest in the holes with which this body gapes.

[31]

Bel Arbre triomphant, victorieux trophée,
Qui pourroit dignement ta loüange entonner?
Au seul ozer ie sens ma Muse s'étonner,
Et ma voix au gosier de frayeur estouffée.

Soy donq, ô digne Croix, toy-mesme ton Orphée,
Et te plaise auiourd'huy piteuse me donner
Qu'à tousiours de ton Nom soit ma gloire étoffée,
Que mon penser ne puisse onques t'abandonner.

Et fay qu'à ce grand iour, qui te verra brillante,
Dans les plaines d'azur, ta lumiere drillante
N'épouuante mon ame, aux pieds de ce vaincueur.

Les marquez à ton coing n'eurent iadis à craindre.
Je ne craindray non plus, s'il te plait de t'empreindre,
Par le burin d'amour, sur le roc de mon cœur.

[61]

Auecques Noëmi, cette chetiue Mere
Aux Dames de Salem disoit ie vous suply,
Ne me dites plus belle, ains m'appelez amere:
La Seigneur a mon cœur d'amertume remply.

Les plus griefues douleurs peintes sur le reply
Des vieux siecles passés reduites en sommaire,
Auprés de ma douleur, ne sont qu'vne Chimere.
Voicy ton Prognostic, ô Vieillard, accomply.

De la mort de mon Fils naist la ferme esperance
Du salut des humains: i'ay fidele asseurance
Que sa mort de la mort le rend ores vainqueur.

Mais son corps qui s'expose à ce martyre extreme
Est à moy, c'est mon sang, il m'est plus que moy-mesme
Ce qu'il souffre en son corps, ie le souffre en mon cœur.

[31]

Fair Tree of triumph, trophy of the fight
Whose song could worthily declare your praise?
At the sheer daring I can feel my muse
Shake, and my voice stick in my throat for fright.

Be therefore your own Orpheus, worthy Cross
Be pleased this day for pity's sake to grant me
Such fame as your name henceforth may increase
Such thoughts of you as evermore may haunt me.

And on that great day which will see you bright
Upon the sky's plains, may your piercing light
Not cause my soul, bowed at his feet, to start.

Those long since marked with your mark had no fear:
No more shall I if you are pleased to score
The rock, with your love's chisel, of my heart.

[61]

'I beg you,' said this Mother with Naomi
To Salem's ladies out of her distress
'No longer call me fair, but bitter say:
The Lord has filled my heart with bitterness.

'The deepest woes depicted on the fold
Of years unfolding, in epitome,
Beside my woe are but a mockery:
Your prophecy, old Simeon, is fulfilled.

'The certain hope is born from my son's death
Of man's salvation, and I have firm faith
That his death makes him now death's conqueror.

'But oh, his body in this agony
Is mine, my blood, more than myself to me:
What he in body bears, in heart I bear.'

[65]

Cependant le Soleil fournissant sa iournée
Voit son Maistre à la Croix de tormens foisonné,
Ja prest à rendre l'ame: il blesmit étonné,
Et volontiers sa course eut ailleurs détournée.

Il se fasche de voir sa teste enuironnée
D'vn brillant diademe, & dit passionné
Dois-je auoir de rayons ma teste couronnée,
Voyant mon Createur d'espines couronné?

A ces mots il arrache auecques violance
Sa flambante couronne, & despité l'élance
Dans les abysmes creux, soudain le iour s'enfuit.

O comme tu sers bien, ô Soleil, ce bon Maistre
Tu fis naistre vn beau iour la nuict, qui le veit naistre
Et ce iour qu'il se meurt tu fais naistre vne nuict.

[77]

Dez qu'il eut dit, I'AY SOIF, vn Iuif prend vne esponge,
L'enuironne d'hyssope, & (suiuant la façon
Des Juifs) dans le vinaigre il la plonge, & replonge,
Et luy porte à la bouche, ô cruelle boisson.

Par cette amere aigreur vous payez la rançon
(Or que sur vous la mort plus ses griffes allonge
O Christ) de la douceur, qui seruit d'hameçon
Pour prendre le vieil Homme, au pere de mensonge.

Mais, las! est-ce le fruit si long temps attendu
Que vous a vostre vigne à ce besoin rendu?
Qui vous la conuertie en lambrusque sauuage?

Il ne restoit plus rien caché dans les replis
De tant d'Oracles vieux, que cet ingrat breuuage.
Jls sont ores en vous tout à fait accomplis.

[65]

Meanwhile the sun, laying out its full glare
Sees its pain-swollen Master on the Cross
Ready to yield his spirit: at a loss
It pales, has gladly moved its course elsewhere.

Seeing a brilliant diadem surround
His head, it fills with grief, with passion burns:
'Am I to have my head with sunbeams crowned
When I see my Creator crowned with thorns?'

So saying it tears off in a violent fit
Its flaming crown, and thwarted tosses it
Into the hollow depths: day takes to flight.

Sun, your good Master's servant proves his worth
Bringing forth day the night that saw his birth
And on his death-day bringing forth a night.

[77]

As soon as he has said 'I thirst', a Jew
Impales a sponge which he has duly sunk
In vinegar until it is soaked through
Upon a stick, holds up the cruel drink.

This is the bitterness that pays the price
(Now that to you death stretches out its claws
O Christ) of sweetness, now a bait to entice
And hook the Old Man from the lord of lies.

Alas! Is this the fruit so long awaited
Is this the need to which your vine is fitted?
Who looked at it that it brought forth wild grapes?

Of all in those old oracles concealed
This only is left, unfolding at your lips:
In you now they are utterly fulfilled.

[78]

Le fievreux au chaud mal, qui sa vie rauage
Traité par cil, qui sçait, & veut le secourir
Va pratiquant par ordre à fin de ne perir
La diete, le suer, le saigner, le breuuage.

La fievre du peché faisoit vn tel rauage
Sur cet homme pecheur, qu'il estoit au mourir:
Christ soumis pour cet Homme au naturel seruage,
A fait ce qu'il deut faire, à fin de le guerir.

Il a quarante iours vescu sans nourriture:
Il sua fort her-soir ores par l'ouuerture
De ses veines, Caluaire est de sang tout remply.

Jl restoit (pour finir cette cure admirable)
Ce breuuage, & le Christ, tout à fait secourable,
Le prend, l'auale, & dit que TOUT EST ACCOMPLY.

[85]

Dez que cette Oraison fut par luy prononcée
Il laisse vn peu sa teste à main droite pancher:
Non tant pour les douleurs dont elle est offensée,
Que pour semondre ainsi la Parque d'approcher.

Voila soudain la peau de son front dessecher,
Voila de ses beaux yeux tout à coup enfoncée
L'vne & l'autre prunele, & leur flamme éclipsée,
Leur paupiere abatuë, & leurs reaux se cacher.

Ses narines à peine estant plus diuisées
Rendent son nez aigu: ses temples sont crusées,
Sur ses levres s'espand la pasleur de la mort.

Son haleine est deux fois perduë, & recouuerte,
A la tierce il expire, auec vn peu d'effort,
Les yeux à demy clos, & la bouche entr'-ouuerte.

[78]

One hot with fever, hard by dissolution
Treated by one who can, will, bring relief
Will as instructed try to save his life
By diet, sweating, letting blood, a potion.

The fever of sin was laying such a waste
To man, this sinner, that his death was near:
Christ for this man in nature's bondage pressed
Has done what he must do to work a cure.

He lived for forty days and did not eat
He sweated through his open veins last night
And Calvary with his let blood is filled.

Remained, to end this wondrous work of healing
This potion: Christ whose help is wholly willing
Takes, swallows it, and says 'All is fulfilled'.

[85]

'Into thy hands . . .': uttering this last prayer
He leans his head a little to the right
Not so much for the pains that rack it, more
A signal, for he summons thus the Fate.

Look, suddenly his forehead's skin goes dry
And his two pupils suddenly glaze over:
Their flame is in eclipse, their lowered lids cover
And quench the fading highlight of each eye.

His nostrils barely any more dilate
But pinch his nose, his temples hollow out:
Across his lips the white of death is cast.

His breathing is twice seen to stop and start:
The third time he struggles to breathe his last
With eyes half open and with lips apart.

[95]

Le Coronnel des Juifs frapant sur le rocher
De sa puissante verge, en fit iaillir vne onde
Pour étancher la soif dont il voyoit secher
Dans l'aride desert sa troupe vagabonde.

Longin n'eut plustost fait cette playe profonde
Dans le flanc, où sa lance osa bien se ficher,
Qu'on en veid reiaillir vn breuuage plus cher,
Vn Nectar dont l'vsage eternise le monde.

Ce Nectar precieux qui coule abondamment
Des arteres du cœur de ce parfait Amant
Est nostre nourriture, & nostre medecine.

Ce doux Nectar attraine vn cristal blanchissant
Dont se forme en l'Eglise vne sainte Piscine
Où se vuide le pus, qui nous suit en naissant.

[96]

Sur cette Catastrophe vn Iuif d'Arimathie
Noble, opulent, & iuste (heureux qui n'auoit pas
Esté du noir Conseil de la gent peruertie)
Pour entomber le Christ fidele haste ses pas.

Jl auoit maintefois sauouré ses apas:
Son ame estoit vers luy dés-ja bien conuertie:
Mais la peur a tousiours contraint la sympathie;
Il ne s'en ose ouurir iusques à ce trespas.

A ce trépas l'amour sur la crainte commande,
Jl aborde asseuré Pilate, & luy demande
Ce Corps mort. Il l'obtient. O Iuif heureux cent fois.

Il va prendre vn linceul, & retourne en Caluaire,
Aidé de Nicodeme, il descend de la Croix
Iesus, & le repose au giron de sa Mere.

[95]

The leader of the Jews, striking the rock
With his most mighty rod, made water burst
In the parched desert that his wandering flock
Whom he saw growing faint might quench their thirst.

Longinus has no sooner made this wound
Deep in Christ's side where his spear dared strike home
When thence a dearer draught is seen to stream
A Nectar bringing to all life without end.

This precious Nectar of the heart, which over-
flows from the arteries of this perfect Lover
Is to us food and physic without want.

Sweet Nectar bringing crystal waters forth
Whose power to clear fills in the Church a font
Draining the pus which follows us from birth.

[96]

Catastrophe. A noble, righteous, rich
Jew of Arimathea (blessed he
Not learning what his warped kin darkly teach)
Hurries to bury Jesus faithfully.

Jesus has charmed him many times: in faith
His soul has long since turned to him. But he
(For fear has ever tempered sympathy)
Dared not reveal himself until this death.

With this death perfect love has cast out fear:
He accosts Pilate boldly, asks him for
This corpse, and (blessed, blessed Jew!) receives him.

He goes off for a sheet, comes back to wrap
Jesus: with Nicodemus' help he gives him
Down from the Cross into his Mother's lap.

[97]

A ce nouuel assaut de l'extreme douleur,
Cette Mere au plus vif de son ame touchée
Demeure froide, & seche, à la Croix attachée,
Le visage couuert d'vne morte pasleur.

Iean son fils adoptif a la mesme couleur,
Et les Dames encor, qui l'auoient approchée:
Dont l'vne fait épaule à sa teste panchée,
L'autre frapant ses mains r'apele sa chaleur.

Tandis grosse de dueil la Sainte débauchée
Sur le corps du Sauueur tient sa veuë fichée,
Sans plaintes à la bouche, & sans larmes aux yeux.

Puis sentant la douleur trop viuement la mordre,
Elle rompt le silence, & se lasche au desordre,
Perçant de pleurs la terre, & de plaintes les Cieux.

[98]

Quelle voy-ie à ce coup (dit-elle) cette face,
Cet obiet desiré des bien-heureux esprits,
Qui toutes les beautez de ce bas monde efface,
Qui serene l'azur de l'étoilé pourpris?

Quels voy-ie ces flambeaux, qui des feux de Cypris
Triomphant, ont mon cœur fait deuenir de glace
A l'amour impudique, à fin de donner place
A l'amour sacre-sainct dont il est ore épris?

Quelles voy-ie ces mains, qui les Cieux massonnerent?
Et quels voy-ie ces pieds, qui les ondes calmerent?
O méchef, ô desordre, ô mer d'afflictions.

O trop fidele Amant, que seul ie porte en l'ame,
Voulez-vous que pour moy tant de perfections
Tapissent desormais sous vne froide lame?

[97]

As a new surge of pain against her breaks
That Mother, touched in her soul's quickest place
Cool and dry-eyed remains, close to the Cross
A deathly pallor spread across her cheeks.

John her adoptive son wears the same hue
The women also, coming to her aid:
One lends a shoulder to her drooping head
Another slaps her hands to bring her to.

Meanwhile the Sinner Saint, pregnant with grief
At her Lord's body cannot gaze enough:
Silent her lips, and without tears her eyes.

Then as the gnawing pain reaches its crisis
She breaks the silence and goes all to pieces
Piercing the earth with tears, the heavens with cries.

[98]

'What face is this,' she says, 'which I see now
This object every blessed spirit desires
Which wipes out all the beauties here below
Which smooths the blue of the abode of stars?

'What torches are these over Venus' fires
Triumphant, which have turned my heart to ice
At unchaste love, that I may yield its place
To sacred love which now my heart adores?

'What hands are these, which gave the heavens their form?
And what these feet I see, which calmed the storm?
Mischance, misrule, O sea of my afflictions!

'Too faithful Lover, in my soul your seed
What about me? Must so many perfections
Grovel henceforth beneath a cold steel blade?'

[99]

Acheuant cette plainte à genoux, elle étreint
Les pieds de son Amant, dont la mort la tormente:
Les relaue des pleurs, que sa douleur épreint,
Et de mille baisers tiedement les fomente.

Joseph, qui voit tandis que ce gros dueil augmente
Par l'aspect de l'obiect, & qui iustement craint
D'estre surpris du temps, se dispose contraint
De retirer ce corps des bras de cette Amante.

Ia Nicodeme auoit aporté des parfums,
Ils l'habillent ainsi que leurs autres defuncts,
Et l'emportent pieux dans le iardin tout proche.

Ils vouloient l'honorer d'vn sepulchre plus beau,
Mais n'ayant le loisir, dans le creux d'vne roche
Jls entombent celuy, qui n'a point de Tombeau.

[100]

Iamais ce creux rocher ne veid dans sa closture
Vn corps mort, il est vierge, il est neuf, c'est raison
De donner à mon Christ (qui toute la nature
En pureté surpasse) vne pure maison.

Mais pourquoy d'aloës, & de myrrhe à foison
Pour embaumer ce corps exempt de pourriture?
Pourquoy tous ces parfums? Quoy leur exhalaison
Est elle necessaire à cette sepulture?

Semon, pour nous aprendre à parfumer nos cœurs
De pensers, de desirs de l'ordure vaincueurs
Pour seruir à ce mort de tombeau venerable.

Defunct, qui seul pouuez nos desirs parfumer
De vos graces, grand Dieu, soyez moy fauorable,
A tant que dans mon cœur ie vous puisse inhumer.

[99]

She clasps, ending this dirge upon her knees
Her Lover's feet, whom grievously she misses
Washes them with more tears which her woes squeeze
Applies a poultice of a thousand kisses.

Joseph, who sees that this great mourning harms
The more its object can be seen, who knows
The sabbath is approaching, anxious goes
To ease this body from its lover's arms.

Already Nicodemus has brought spices:
They dress him as with all their dead their use is
And bear him to his nearby garden grave.

They wanted him to have a fairer room
But being short of time, inside a cave
They lay to rest the one who has no tomb.

[100]

This hollow rock by death was never haunted:
Virgin it is and new, and that is why
As an untainted house it has been granted
To Christ, who passes nature's purity.

But why these aloes, all this myrrh to embalm
This body, which corruption shall not see?
Why all these spices? Why is their sweet perfume
So necessary to this exequy?

Let us sow, teaching our hearts to be sweet
Thoughts and desires that lead to filth's defeat
Setting for this dead one a worthy place.

You who alone can fragrant grace impart
To our desires, dead God, look on my face
That I may bury you within my heart.

Seconde Partie
Premier Liure

Second Part
First Book

[1]

I'ay chanté le Combat, la Mort, la sepulture
Du Christ qu'on a comblé de torts iniurieux:
Je chante sa descente aux antres stygieux
Pour tirer noz ayeulx de leur noire closture.

Je chante (émerueillé) comme sans ouuerture
De sa Tombe, il en sort viuant, victorieux.
Ie chante son Triomphe: & l'effort glorieux
Dont il guinda là haut l'vne & l'autre Nature.

Clair Esprit, dont ma Muse a cy-deuant apris
Ses douleurs, ses tourmens, sa honte, & son mespris,
Faites qu'or' de sa gloire elle soit étofée.

Sus, Vierge, il faut tarir les torrens de vos pleurs,
Ie veux (si vous m'aidez) éleuer son Trophée,
Et guirlander son chef de mille & mille fleurs.

[5]

Les escadrons aislez du celeste pourpris
Par le Pere choisis des bandes Coronnelles,
Ialoux d'executer les charges paternelles
Accompagnent le Fils au voyage entrepris.

Aprochans les cachots des rebelles esprits
Ils vont criant aux Roys des ombres criminelles,
Ouurez à ce grand Roy vos portes eternelles,
Puis qu'il a rançonné les siens à si grand prix.

C'ét le Roy de la Gloire il faut, il faut qu'il entre:
Tout l'Auerne croulant du comble iusqu'au centre,
Troublé respond, quel est ce Prince glorieux?

C'ét le Seigneur tresfort, repliquent les bons Anges,
Tres-puissant au combat, tousiours victorieux,
Dont les Cieux & la terre annoncent les loüanges.

[1]

I have sung the battle, death and burial
Of Christ insulted, overwhelmed with wrong:
His harrowing of the Styx is now my song
To draw our fathers out of their black cell.

I sing the unopened tomb, amazed I cry
His coming out alive, victorious:
I sing his triumph, sing the glorious
Power that hoisted both his natures high.

Bright Spirit from whom my muse before has learned
How he was hurt and tortured, shamed and scorned
Let her be wound now in his glory's toils:

Get up, girl, dry the torrents of your tears
For if you help me I will raise his spoils
And wreathe his head in a thousand thousand flowers.

[5]

The wingèd squadrons of the heavenly hall
Picked by the Father from the topmost bands
Eager to carry out their Lord's commands
Fly with the Son as he sets out for hell.

They reach the hideouts of the rebel host
Criminal shades whose kings hear their shouts ring:
'Open your eternal gates to this great King
Who has redeemed his own at such great cost!

'He is the King of glory, he must come in!'
From pole to centre Hades' domes begin
To crumble: 'Who is the Prince so glorious?'

'He is the Lord,' the good angels reply
'Mighty in battle, ever victorious
Whose praises are declared by earth and sky.'

[26]

Si la nature peut aux morts rendre la vie,
L'Autheur de la nature est encor plus puissant,
Le ver meurt dans son nid, & sa mort est suiuie
De la vie, qui va de sa mort renaissant.

Quand pour la mort des siens la douleur va pressant
Le triste Pelican, son amour le conuie
A s'ouurir la poictrine, & son sang jaillissant
Les r'auiue, & leur vie assouuit son enuie,

L'Aigle se r'ajeunit par sa propre vertu,
Le serpent dans le trou de sa peau deuestu,
Se r'emplace, en sortant, de ce qu'il abandonne,

Hé pourquoy, reprouuez, ne croyez vous donc pas,
Qu'ores le Pere au Fils céte vie redonne,
Et qu'il nous face encor viure apres le trépas?

[35]

L'oyseau dont l'Arabie a fait si grande feste,
Est de ce grand Heros le symbole asseuré.
Le Phenix est tout seul: Le Christ est figuré
Seul libre entre les morts par son Royal Prophete.

Le Phenix courageux se porte à sa defaite
Sur du bois parfumé: l'Amour démesuré
Fait que Christ a la mort sur ce bois enduré,
Qui parfume le Ciel d'vne odeur tres-parfaicte.

De sa moüelle apres le Phenix rénaissant
Enleue tout son bois, & l'emporte puissant
Sur vn Autel voisin des arenes brulées.

Par sa Diuinité le Christ resuscitant,
Sur l'azuré lambris des voutes estoillées
Esleuera son bois de rayons éclatant.

[26]

If nature can give life back to the dead
How much more mighty is nature's Origin:
The silkworm dies in its cocoon, its head
Emerges as a moth's head, born again.

When for its dying brood it pines for grief
The melancholy pelican for love
Tears at its breast, whose blood gushes relief
For them, and it is glad for what it gave.

The eagle by its own virtue is renewed
The lurking serpent is afresh endued
With skin, crawls out and leaves the old aside:

Why not believe, then, you of little faith
The Father has restored the Son who died
And makes us live again after our death?

[35]

The bird so much esteemed by Araby
Is this great hero's sure and certain sign.
The phoenix is unique: Christ is alone
Among the dead, as David promised, free.

The phoenix bravely goes off to its doom
On fragrant wood: and boundless love has led
Christ to endure his death upon this wood
Which sweetens heaven with the best perfume.

The phoenix from its marrow born again
Takes all its wood, lays it with might and main
Upon an altar near the burning sands:

Christ by his godhead, death's ordeal now ended
High in the starry vault's blue ceiling stands
Raising his wood to be a beam all splendid.

[43]

Ce grand Soleil, de qui l'autre n'est qu'vne flame
Par quatre des maisons du grand Cercle a passé.
Par celle de la Vierge, où neuf mois sa belle ame
A de son corps égal l'organe compassé.

Par celle du Vers'eau, quand son œil a trassé
Sa douleur par son pleur, en maint acte sans blasme,
Par celle du Taureau, quand son corps terrassé
S'est pour victime offert sur le gibet infame.

Or à ce iour il entre en celle du Lion
Perruqué de lumiere, il darde vn milion
De rayons flamboyans sur les deux Hemispheres,

Et sa voix rugissante, & son fremissement
Au sortir de la tombe espouuantent les feres,
Et les rangent au ioug de leur amandement.

[50]

Le Cerf que le veneur relance au bois sauuage,
Void vn fleuue, s'y iette, nage, & gaigne le bord.
Christ poursuiuy de Juifs, nage aux eaux de la mort,
Les passe, & vient surgir à l'immortel riuage.

Le Cerf hayt le serpent, l'attaque, le rauage,
Le mord & l'engloutit: Christ mortellement mord
Le serpent qui fournit à la mort son breuuage:
Céte mort engloutit, & destruict son effort.

Il a (pource qu'il est le viuant & la vie)
Céte mort deuorée à son estre asseruie,
Comme l'estomach change en lait son aliment.

A ce victorieux la trompe prophetique
Comme au Cerf matineux a chanté son Cantique
Et nous semond fidele au mesme compliment.

[43]

This Sun of whom the other is one flame
Has passed through four signs of the mighty Wheel:
That of the Virgin when nine months his frame
Was rounded fittingly by his fair soul

That of the Waterbearer when his eye
Traced out in tears kind acts that earned him blame
That of the Bull which saw his body die
A willing victim of the gallows' shame.

He enters now this day that of the Lion
For maned with light he shoots forth by the million
Beams to inflame the world from east to west:

His roaring and his rising cause a movement
That strikes fear in the heart of every beast
And bends it to the yoke of its improvement.

[50]

The stag the huntsman runs from copse and cover
Beholds a river, dives, and shoreward swims:
Christ hounded by the Jews swims in death's streams
Climbs up the far bank, death being now passed over.

The stag, hating the serpent, does its worst,
Bites, swallows it: Christ deals a mortal bite
To this serpent whose venom slakes death's thirst
Swallows this death and drains away its might.

He who is life, and the one left alive
Has to himself made eaten death a slave
As into milk the stomach turns its food

And to this victor the prophetic horn
Has sung its verse as to the Stag at Morn
And faithful summons us to gratitude.

Vœu pour la fin de ce Livre

Intelligible sphere, il est indubitable
Que ton centre est par tout, qu'à luy tout aboutit,
Et le Ciel, & la terre, & l'Enfer redoutable,
Et la tombe, où la mort ta surface abatit.

Mon ame s'en écarte, & pource elle patit;
Et veut s'en approcher: mais l'appast détestable
De céte volupté, faussement delectable,
Par mille obiects trompeurs tousiours l'en diuertit.

Ne vueille plus souffrir que rien l'en diuertisse:
Au centre (où tout se rend) fay qu'ore elle aboutisse,
R'auiue la soudain par ton r'auiuement.

Donne luy tant d'Amour pour te faire adherance
Qu'il passe par de là tout humain iugement,
Comme on ne peut iuger de ta circonferance.

Prayer to end this Book

Intelligible sphere, there is no doubt
Your centre is everywhere, all things are drawn
To end there – heaven and earth, the dreadful pit
And the tomb, where death broke your surface down.

My soul is stricken, she has gone astray:
She wants to draw near, but the loathsome charm
Of all this pleasure always lures to harm
And with a thousand toys turns her away.

Please suffer no things more that wayward tend
And at the centre of all things make her end
Bringing her suddenly to life again:

Give her so much love through your influence
That love exceeds all reckoning of men
As none may reckon your circumference.

Seconde Partie
Second Liure

Second Part
Second Book

De céte verité la preuue veritable
Ayant par trois des sens couru legerement:
Par l'oüye, & la veüe, & par l'attouchement,
Ores par le quatriéme est faicte indubitable.

La cinquieme la rend du tout non disputable:
Car les corps glorieux (mais plus parfaictement
Celuy du Christ depuis le clair r'auiuement)
Parfument l'odorat d'vn parfum delectable.

Ainsi que la Baleine odorante en sa faim
Par son odeur attire, & prend auec cét haim
Mille, & mille poissons dont elle fait curée:

Le Christ attire ainsi par la soüefue odeur
De son corps reuiuant, céte troupe égarée,
Pour saouler de ce mets son amoureuse ardeur.

[84]

He lives. This truth at last is demonstrated:
Having by now within three senses reach
Tripped lightly, that of hearing, sight and touch
It meets the fourth and must no more be doubted.

As for the fifth, there is no argument
For glorious bodies (but above all here
for his own since he was raised up bright and clear)
that faculty with a sweet scent
se monstrous appetite
And battens on a oususes it for bait
housand fish

So Christ by his raised body's fragrant smell
Attracts this wandering flock, and with this dish
The great fire of his yearning has its fill.

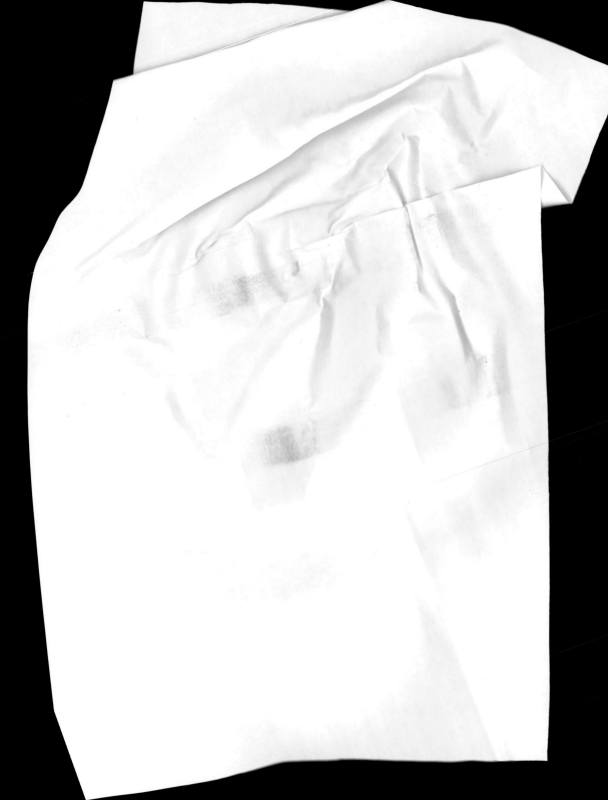

Seconde Partie
Troisieme Liure

Second Part
Third Book

[11]

Ce Beau, par la grandeur de sa vertu, remonte
Sur l'Azuré lambris des Palais radieux
Et par la force encor' de son corps glorieux
Qui le pezant effort de nos elements dompte.

La veüe de chacun des assistans est prompte
A le suiure par l'air: les plus deuotieux
L'accompaignent plus haut: mais cét oeil tres-pieux
De sa Mere en cecy tous les autres surmonte.

Quand de le voir tout autre a perdu le pouuoir,
L'œil de Marie peut & le suiure, & le voir:
Et le suit, & le voit jusques à l'empyrée.

Ainsi que la gigante attache êtroictement
Son amoureuse vmbelle au char de son Amant,
Iusques qu'il ait fondu dans l'azur de Nerée.

[25]

Des citadins du ciel plus que ie ne pourroy
Nombrer, Et quatre d'eux auec quatre cornetes,
Et mille autres sonnant des tambours, des trompetes
En liesse, en triomphe, accompagnent ce Roy.

Ce triomphateur donque auecque le charroy
Du subiect glorieux de ses riches conquestes,
Approche son Olympe en ce pompeux arroy,
Où pour le receuoir toutes choses sont prestes.

Tous les douze portaux de Salem sont ouuers,
Chacun vient hommager ce Roy de l'vniuers,
Dont la teste de neige a des feux aux prunelles.

Jl paruient à la fin iusqu'à l'Ayeul des iours,
Qui doublant (s'il se peut) ses ioyes eternelles,
Donne à son fils la gloire, & l'Empire à tousiours.

[11]

This Fair One, thanks to his great virtue, mounts
Towards the shining palaces' blue ceiling
And with his glorious body's strength sends reeling
The dull resistance of our elements.

The eyes of all those present do their best
To follow him, reaching a greater height
The greater their devotion: but the sight
Of pious Mary outreaches all the rest.

When he is lost from all the others' view
His Mother's eye can track him through the blue
And does so still, up to the topmost sphere

Just as the sunflower for love will ever
Cling to the chariot of the sun her lover
Till the Aegean makes him disappear.

[25]

Townsmen of heaven beyond my reckoning
Ever, and four of them with four cornetts
A thousand others playing drums, trumpets
Blissful, triumphant, marching with this King

This conquering hero bearing on his way
Spoils won because of all the just he spared
Mounts his Olympus in this rich array
Where to receive him all has been prepared

All the twelve gates of Salem are flung wide
This Lord of all by all is magnified
Whose snowy head has fireballs in his eyes

He comes at last up to the Ancient of days
Who doubling (can it be?) his eternal joys
Gives him the glory, the Empire for always.

Seconde Partie
Quatrieme Liure

Second Part
Fourth Book

[1]

Esprit qui fecondez les ames les plus seches,
Qui rendez eloquents les plus rudes espris,
Dardez or sur ma teste vne de voz flammeches,
Et rendez la Ceppede à bien parler apris.

Non pas pour déchifrer ce que n'ont pas compris
Les cerueaux mieux timbrés, j'esquiue ces hauts préches
De vostre PROCEDER. Ie n'ay point entrepris
(Cognoissant qui ie suis) de si grandes dépeches.

Mais bien·pour enseigner au peuple moins sçavant,
Comme en forme de langue, & de flamme, & de vent
Vous estez descendu sur la trouppe fidele.

Secondez mon dessein, & mon cœur façonnez
Sur les traicts plus naïfs de son iuste modele,
A fin de receuoir les dons que vous donnez.

[6]

Nous aprenons aussi de céte vehemence
La presence de Dieu, qui coustumierement
Nous marque les efforts de sa grandeur immense
Par des signes bruyants mysterieusement.

Non pourtant qu'il s'vnisse hypostatiquement
A ces corps (le seul Verbe a faict céte accointance)
Jls luy seruent icy d'enseigne seulement.
Jl resoud quand il veut leur visible existance.

L'Esprit sainct à l'abord est vn peu violent
Pour émouuoir les cœurs: mais il est consolant
Au progez: puis en fin les comble de liesse.

Le malin au contraire arriue doucement
Pour nous amadoüer: mais en fin il nous laisse
Remplis de dueil, de trouble, & d'épouuantement.

[1]

Spirit who make the driest souls bear fruit
Whose eloquence the roughest minds can fill
My head awaits one of your sparks: oh shoot! –
Make La Ceppède adept at speaking well

Not to unravel what a higher college
Has failed to grasp (I dodge those lofty speeches
Concerning your Procession: my self-knowledge
Prevents my drafting such august dispatches)

But to teach folk of the unlearned kind
How in the form of tongues, of flames, of wind
You have descended on your faithful creatures

Support my purpose, fashion now my heart
After its righteous model's simpler features
In order to receive the gifts you impart.

[6]

Vehemence teaches us the works of God:
We learn from it his presence, for his way
To make his mighty power known abroad
Is with great noises that attest his sway.

Yet it is not that he is consubstantial
With bodies, for the Logos is but one:
Rather, these are but signs and circumstantial
Which he melts back to naught when he has done.

The Holy Spirit sets out with violence
To woo the heart, but after he relents
And finally consoles and fills with bliss:

Meanwhile the evil one leads into error
With soft persuasion, moving on from this
To cram us with confusion, woe and terror.

[7]

Aux Prophetes jadis céte Tierce personne
Communiquoit ses dons par le bas sifflement
D'vn petit ventelet: mais ore elle raisonne
Par le souffle d'vn vent actif, & vehement.

Elle ne donnoit lors que bien écharsement
Ses biens: mais soubs le Christ, elle nous en foisonne:
Lors donc à petit bruict: maintenant elle sonne
Bien haut, pour nous marquer qu'elle y va largement.

Des Prophetes l'oreille estoit bien disposée,
Pource il leur suffisoit qu'vne voix reposée
Leur marquat doucement ce qu'ils deuoient sçavoir.

Mais nostre oreille sourde à besoin du tonnerre,
L'Esprit donc que le Christ répand or' sur la terre
Pour nous (apres les siens) bruit pour nous émouuoir.

[9]

Ces langues (dit S. Luc) paroissent départies,
Ce n'est pas que chacune ait vn mi-partement
(Comme on croit des serpens les langues mi-parties)
Mais pource que chacune à son département.

Sur chacun des presents chacune ouuertement
Vient s'asseoir, & rend si prompt aux reparties
Contre les argumens des ames peruerties,
Que les plus obstinez cederont promptement.

Cét Esprit voirement n'est qu'vn: mais il partage
Diuersement ses dons: l'vn en a dauantage,
L'autre moins, & chacun a son contentement.

La figure qu'il prent des langues les engage
A croire qu'il sera leur feal truchement
Tout par tout ou Babel varia le langage.

[7]

To the prophets this Third Person used to make
His gifts known by soft whispers, he would send
A gentle breeze: but now when he will speak
There is a gust, a rushing mighty wind.

But sparingly in those days did he spill
His bounty: under Christ, he showers us.
A little noise then: now a ringing voice
To show us he goes to it with a will.

The ancient prophets' ears were well attuned
So they were happy with a still, small sound
To bring the message home, not loud yet clear:

But our deaf ears have need of thunder, hence
The Spirit Christ spreads over continents
(After his own) must roar to make us hear.

[9]

These tongues appear divided, says St Luke:
This does not mean that each one has a cleft
(Like, we are told, the cleft tongue of the snake)
But that each is divided as a gift.

On each man present each tongue unconcealed
Comes and sits down, and makes each man so quick
To counter any ingenious heretic
That the most obstinate will quickly yield.

This Spirit indeed is One, but of his store
He variously divides: one man has more
Another less, and each has his full share.

Taking the shape of tongues he thus binds each
To trust him as the true interpreter
Wherever Babel has divided speech.

[11]

Ces langues sont de feu. Le feu rend tributaires
Toutes choses à soy. Cent, & cent maux diuers
Sont gueris par le feu, nos vnze en sont couuerts.
Ces langues, & ce feu marquent des grands mysteres.

O vous qui de l'Olympe estes les secretaires,
Qui portez sa parole en ce bas vniuers,
Vos langues doiuent estre autant de forts cauteres,
Pour extirper des cœurs mille vices peruers.

Sus embesougnez donc vos langues allumées,
Pour rendre viuement les ames enflammées
De ce feu, dont le Christ vint la terre allumer.

De peu nous seruiroient vos harangues frequentes,
Vous auriez pour neant des langues eloquentes,
Si vous n'auiez ce feu pour nos cœurs enflammer.

[14]

Le feu de sa nature (agilement fuyante)
Monte, & ne descend point: mais si le peut-on veoir
Descendre quelquefois par le secret pouuoir
D'vn subject qui contient vne cause attrayante.

Du flambeau qu'on esteint la vapeur tournoyante
Va recherchant le feu qu'elle veut receuoir,
Et l'approchant l'attire, & la flamme ondoyante
Descend iusqu'au plus bas, qui le peut conceuoir.

Par l'abscence du Christ, comme lampes esteintes
Les Apostres fumoient, leurs vapeurs ont atteintes
Les flammeches du Ciel, qui descendent sur eux.

Tousiours leur bouche ouuerte exhaloit la fumée
Qui cét esprit attire, & qui rend parfumée
Celle des encensoirs des esprits bien-heureux.

[11]

Of fire, these tongues, fire that makes all things pay
Tribute to it. A hundred different ills
Are cured by fire, and our eleven it fills.
These tongues, this fire mark a great mystery.

O you who are Olympus' secretaries
Who are his spokesmen in this lower sphere
Your tongues must be so many cauteries
That hearts of many vices may be clear.

Up now, employ your kindled tongues and come
Quickly to set all earthly hearts aflame
With that fire Christ came upon earth to start:

Of small avail to us all your harangues
And vainly would you wag your rousing tongues
If you had no fire to inflame the heart.

[14]

Fire by its flickering nature's nimble laws
Goes up, not down: and yet it can occur
That fire goes down, drawn by the secret power
Of bodies dowered with an attractive cause.

If we put out a torch, its swirling smoke
Goes searching for the fire that it would catch
Luring it: then the flame will leap and take
A downward path, where it will meet its match.

With Christ gone, like so many lamps put out
The Apostles smoking stood, but their smoke sought
The sparks of heaven, which on them came to rest:

Their open mouths kept breathing out the fumes
That draw this Spirit and fill with sweet perfumes
The censers of the spirits of the blest.

[17]

Quand la main du Potier artistement agile
A façonné les pots, il les seche, & les cuit
Dans la fournaise ardente: estant fort bien instruit
Que le feu peut (sans autre) affermir son argile.

Ce Potier qui nous fit de matiere fragile,
Desireux d'affermir l'homme qu'il a produit,
A ce coup sur son chef céte flamme conduit,
Pour le cuire au fourneau de son chaud Euangile.

Ie parle de cet homme vniuerselement:
Car ce feu n'est pas propre aux vnze seulement,
Il a couuert maint autre en sa forme visible.

En l'inuisible encor maint autre l'a receu.
D'en faire la demande il est à tous loisible,
Qui le demandera ne sera point deceu.

[23]

Adam forma iadis maint & maint synonyme,
Qui seruit, comme on dit, aux langages diuers:
Mais ce confus jargon fut la peine du crime
Du peuple, qui resté répeupla l'vniuers.

Le Sauueur assemblant les bons, & les peruers
En corps d'Eglise, veut qu'ores elle s'exprime
En des termes qui soint à chacun découuers
A fin qu'aux cœurs de tous, sa doctrine s'imprime.

Ce donc, que la superbe obscur auoit rendu,
L'humilité le rend maintenant entendu,
Toute langue à sa source est comme revnie

Ie dy, comme, d'autant que la vraye vnité
Du langage d'Heber, promise en Sophonie
Ne sera qu'au seiour de la Diuinité.

[17]

When the skilled potter in his nimble way
Has shaped his work, he dries and bakes each pot
In the fiery furnace, for he has been taught
That fire is all he needs to strengthen clay.

This Potter who formed us, so early fallen
Wishing to strengthen man whom he had made
At this guided this flame on to his head
To bake it well in his hot Gospel's kiln.

I mean by this man all men under heaven
For this fire is not privy to the eleven:
Many more it has covered visibly

To many more again it has been granted
Unseen. To ask for it all men are free:
Whoever asks will not be disappointed.

[23]

Adam once shaped many a synonym
Which is, some say, why tongues are so diverse:
But this confused speech punished Babel's crime
Whose criminals now fill the universe.

The Saviour gathering all, both good and ill
Into the Church, desires that she declare
In terms that to all nations shall reveal
His teaching, touching all hearts everywhere.

This, which pride hitherto had made obscure
Is understood by all whose hearts are pure
And all tongues to their source are now united

Even as the promised unity, I say
Of Heber's tongue, as Zephaniah indited
Shall be but till the godhead comes to stay.

Notes

The poet's original notes, far more extensive than what follows, were designed primarily to demonstrate his orthodoxy to a France torn by wars of religion. Whether or not the need for them contributed to the allusive style of the sonnets, that style makes notes as necessary as ever.

As in the Introduction, a reference like *1:3:20* means Part 1, Book 3, Sonnet 20. References to the New Testament narrative are given as Mt (Matthew), Mk (Mark), L (Luke), J (John), A (Acts), followed by the chapter number. Biblical quotations are in the King James version (KJ) because it is the most familiar, with frequent references to the Vulgate (Vg) which the poet has used. Notes with English headwords are for all readers; notes with French headwords are for readers of the original.

Contents
prinse: *prise*; from *prehensam*.
de Caluaire: *du Calvaire*.
vœu: in the etymological sense of *votum* 'votive offering, prayer'.
dépuis: *dès*; cf Spanish *después*.
icelle: *celle(-là)*; from *hic illam*.
iusques qu'il monta: *jusqu'à ce qu'il montât*.

Foreword: To France
discourent: a rare transitive use, like Hamlet's recorder (Act 3, Scene 2) which 'will discourse most eloquent music'.
admiration: in the etymological sense of 'staring at'.
pourtrait: past participle of old *portraire*, from *protrahere* 'to draw forth'.
immortalisé: *immortalisés*.
agreoit: *-ois* etc. was the imperfect ending, pronounced *wè* (from *-abam* etc.); it rhymed with *rois* (*rwè*). During the 17th century *wè* as a verb ending became *è*, elsewhere *wa*, but spelling did not reflect the change until the 18th century.
ores . . . ores: 'now . . . now'; cf *or*, *d'ores et déjà*.
le retour des années la veüe du depuis: . . . *l'a vue depuis*.
si qu'au lieu d'estre tousiours: 'indeed . . .'; from *sic*.
caute: 'cautious', who *cavet*.
ie la demasqué, & recognu: *je la démasquai, et reconnus*.
& la chasser: *et de la chasser*.
ains: *mais (plutôt)*; from *ante*. The final *s* was pronounced.
harlot: 'and the Lord said to Hosea, Go, take unto thee a wife of whoredoms and

children of whoredoms: for the land hath committed great whoredom, departing from the Lord. So he went and took Gomer . . . which conceived, and bare him a son. And the Lord said unto him, Call his name Jezreel' (Hosea 1).

a foreigner and a captive: 'when thou goest forth to war against thine enemies, and the Lord thy God hath delivered them into thy hands, and thou . . . seest among the captives a beautiful woman, and . . . thou wouldest have her to be thy wife; then . . . she shall shave her head . . . and she shall put the raiment of her captivity from off her' (Deuteronomy 21).

raire: *raser*.

two-edged razor: recalling John the Divine's vision of the 'sharp twoedged sword' emerging from Christ's mouth (Revelation 1).

Ethnique: Greek *ethnos* is Latin *gens* (and Hebrew *goy*).

monstreux: *monstrueux*.

mal-heurs: hyphenated because *heur* was still remembered as a noun meaning 'luck' (from *augurium*).

cettuy-cy: *celui-ci*; *cettuy* (*cestui*, *cétui*) is from *hic *istui*.

Prophet: Ezekiel, whose Vision included a hand bearing a scroll 'written within and without' (Ezekiel 2).

pour ce: *pour cette raison*. Sometimes written *pource*; cf 'therefore'. As a conjunction, *pource que* is *parce que*.

seurant: *sevrant*.

aussi-tost que i'ay peu: . . . *pu*.

arguer: three syllables, *accuser*.

1:1:6 Mt26, Mk14, L22, J18.

Amphions: Amphion was a son of Zeus who with the music of his lyre rebuilt the walls of Thebes.

despartir: *se départir*.

foreign: in his Foreword (q.v.) the poet argues that poetry, being by nature sacred and immortal, is more at home with sacred and immortal themes.

Timanthes: plural here like 'Amphions' above, Timanthes was a Greek painter of the 4th century BC.

Amatonte: Amathus, a shrine in Cyprus dedicated to Aphrodite (Venus) and Adonis.

1:1:21 Mt26, Mk14.

Rachel: wife of Jacob. 'And it came to pass, as her soul was in departing, (for she died) that she called his name Ben-oni; but his father called him Benjamin' (Genesis 35). KJ glosses Ben-oni 'the son of my sorrow'.

s'accoucha: *accoucha*.

valeur: in the etymological sense of 'health' (*valorem*, from *valere* 'to be well').

s'écoulantes: *s'écoulant*.

Christ: *le Christ*.

sorrowful unto death: 'my soul is exceeding sorrowful unto death', quoted in the translation because the original refers to a sonnet not translated.

ià desia: a reinforced *déjà*.

1:1:29 Mt26, Mk14, L22.

cloud-piercing ray: 'the prayer of the humble pierceth the clouds' (Ecclesiasticus 35).

ne se parque . . . n'esleue (élève): modern French would require a supporting *pas* or equivalent.

c'il (more correctly elsewhere *cil*): *celui*; from *hic illum*.

surgeonne: 'puts out suckers', suggesting that the water is bubbling up here and there.

emmy: *parmi*; from *in medio*. Linguistically this sonnet is one of the most archaic.

n'en peut . . . contenter: *ne peut en contenter*.

your water: recalling Jesus' meeting at the well with the woman of Samaria, whom he asked for a drink and to whom he offered 'living water' (J4).

1:1:38 L22.

premier: *d'abord*.

humeur: in the etymological sense of *humorem* 'moisture'; cf 'humidity'.

vuider: *vider*; cf 'void'.

1:1:48 Mt26, Mk14, L22, J18.

priuauté: *intimité*.

your task: as treasurer (J13).

owls: a traditional emblem of the Jews, who prefer the dark although the Light has come.

haineuse: *haïssable*.

1:1:79 Mt26, Mk14.

hazarde: *jette par hasard*.

cependant: *pendant*.

coüarde: *lâche*. 'Showing one's tail' (*queue*, from *caudam*); cf 'coward'.

glu: curiously changes gender in the last line.

stone: the poet recalls the 'spiritual Rock' (also *pierre*) of Christ in 1 Corinthians 10. Still more appropriate is 'the stone which the builders rejected' of Psalm 118 (Vg 117) quoted in Mt21, Mk12, L20.

1:1:88 Mk14.

linceul: 'sheet' (from *linteolum* 'piece of linen') has since come to mean only 'winding-sheet'; cf the semantic progress of Vg *sindon*, taken from the Greek original and possibly of Indian origin ('muslin'), for the KJ 'linen cloth' out of which the young man (sometimes identified with the Evangelist) slipped at Jesus' arrest.

rauie: shows concord by position.

habits: the poet says he intends the word both literally and 'allegorically'; cf *Avant-Propos*: *pour luy descoudre ses mondains habits (ou plustost habitudes)*.

1:1:91 Mt26, Mk14, L22, J18.

trauaillez: in the old sense; cf 'travail'.

griefs: in the old sense, as in English.

peineux: *pénibles*.

haineux: *ennemis*.

estreintes: in the wider sense of 'pressures'.

espreintes: in the wider sense of 'squeezings'.

1:1:96

Samson: the strong man of Judges 16, born to 'begin to deliver' Israel from the

Philistines, for which purpose he took the Nazirite ('consecrated') vows of abstinence from all produce of the vine and of leaving his hair uncut (Numbers 6). Christianity has often confused the terms Nazirite and Nazarene, which may explain Jesus' refusal to drink wine at Passover (L22).

fuitifs: fugitifs.

fugitives: accidental killers for whose refuge six cities were set aside until the death of the high priest, when they could return home (Numbers 35).

pollus: pollués; an old past participle, from *pollutos.*

Jsacide: an adjective formed from *Isaac*; cf *Sionides (1:2:73)*, and *1:3:24.*

1:1:99

on la fait prisonnier: la is *l'a.*

vefuage: veuvage.

feconde: fécondant?

esmail: émail, conventional term for vernal hues.

alme: 'life-giving'; cf *Alma Mater.*

Dew: 'I will be as the dew unto Israel: he shall grow as the lily, and cast forth his roots as Lebanon' (Hosea 14).

1:2:41   Mt26, Mk14, L22, J18.

friandise: the appetite rather than its gratification.

marchandise: the activity rather than its product.

la Lote: le lotus, according to the poet.

viande: in the etymological sense of *vivenda* 'victuals'; cf KJ 'meat'.

1:2:44   J18.

cependant: in the old sense of 'meanwhile' ('during this').

l'hypocrite ressemble . . .: these lines are oddly reminiscent of the last stanza of *l'Albatros* by Baudelaire.

ostrich: the bird's association with hypocrisy is traditional, says the poet, and possibly due to its being ritually unclean. (See Leviticus 11; KJ wrongly has 'owl'.)

1:2:54

white: the poet characteristically gives chapter and verse for each item.

par mesme raison: pour la même raison.

pontiff: Aaron, Moses' brother, the first Israelite priest (Leviticus 16).

s'affeubloit: s'affublait.

deüe: due.

1:2:63   Mt27, Mk15, J19.

This and the following two sonnets form a triptych on the emblems of Christ's kingship.

trait: past participle of *traire*, in the etymological sense of *trahere* 'draw'.

Carmes: from *carmina* 'songs, poems'. A learned derivation; cf *charmes.*

daigne toy de cacher: daigne cacher.

brindelles: brindilles.

1:2:64

bramble: recalling God's reproach to Israel as an unproductive vineyard (Isaiah 5).

crimineuses: *incriminantes*.
punishment: for man's first disobedience (Genesis 3).
coulpe: from *culpam* 'fault'.
burning bush: in which God appeared to Moses (Exodus 3).
seiour: the abode rather than the time spent there.
cet halier: *ce hallier*.

1:2:65
the wondrous skill: an ancient belief.
that serpent: Satan.
dextre: *main droite*.
gentile: 'and all the inhabitants of Egypt shall know that I am the Lord, because
    they have been a staff of reed to the house of Israel' (Ezekiel 29).
suis-ie pas: such a construction is frowned on even today; contrast the archaic
    unsupported *ne* of *1:1:29*. (*Pas* after *ne* was originally a noun: *je ne marche pas*.)
flattened: recalling Jesus' taunt to the crowd after the arrest of John the
    Baptist: 'What went ye out into the wilderness to see? A reed shaken with the
    wind?' (Mt11, L7). Weeks before the poet died, Pascal was born: 'Man is but
    a reed, nature's weakest; but he is a thinking reed' (*Pensées* 6:347).

1:2:67   Mt27, Mk15, J19.
This and the following sonnet form a closely related pair.
lover of my soul: following a Christian interpretation of the Song of Songs.
douleureux: *douloureux*.

1:2:68
blind man: whose sight Jesus restored with clay made from spittle (J9).

1:2:69   Mt27, Mk15, L23, J19.
This and the following two sonnets form an *Ecce homo* triptych.
foruoyantes: *se fourvoyant*.
therefore be . . . at these words: a rare example for the period of the rhetorical
    figure aposiopesis ('falling silent', one sentence interrupted by another), rare
    enough for the poet to invoke Virgil as his model.

1:2:70
sanglantez: *ensanglantés*.
test (*têt*): *crâne*. *Tête* is from *testam* 'pot', *têt* from *testum* 'lid'.

1:2:71
image: sometimes masculine in a religious context in pre-Classical French.
œuure: still reflects the gender ambiguity of its origin (*opera*, neuter plural
    interpreted as feminine singular).
Rachel: who on leaving her father Laban after his quarrel with her husband
    Jacob, stole his idols 'and sat upon them. And Laban searched all the tent,
    but found them not. And she said to her father, Let it not displease my Lord
    that I cannot rise up before thee; for the custom of women is upon me'
    (Genesis 31). One of the poet's more ingenious parallels.

1:2:72
the old man: Jacob. 'And it came to pass . . . that Reuben went and lay with

Bilhah his father's concubine' (Genesis 35). 'Reuben . . . thou shalt not excel; because thou wentest up to thy father's bed' (Genesis 49).

nourriture: nourrisson.

ce puant la poluë: la is *l'a; poluë* is a past participle (cf *1:1:96, 1:2:44*).

Ham: a son of Noah who 'saw the nakedness of his father' (Genesis 9).

1:2:73

daughters of Zion: 'go forth, O ye daughters of Zion, and behold king Solomon' (Song of Songs 3).

more than Solomon: recalling Jesus' description of himself as 'a greater than Solomon' (Mt12).

creus: crûs.

Bethel: from Hebrew *bêth 'el* 'house of God', after the place where God spoke to Jacob (Genesis 35).

1:2:85   J19.

no king . . .: quoted in the translation because the original refers to a sonnet not translated.

adueu: aveu.

oracle: 'the sceptre shall not depart from Judah . . . until Shiloh come' (Genesis 49). The Vg renders the obscure Shiloh 'he who is to be sent'.

Messiah: like many Christians, the poet seems to derive the word from *missum* 'sent'. It comes in fact from Hebrew *māshîcha* 'anointed', in Greek *christos.*

s'escrians: s'écriant.

Paran: the desert area north of Mt Sinai, where scouts sent into the promised land reported to the Israelites that 'surely it floweth with milk and honey . . . nevertheless the people be strong that dwell in the land, and the cities are walled, and very great' (Numbers 13); whereupon they 'murmured against Moses' and resolved what the poet quotes (Numbers 14).

1:3:10   Mt27, Mk15, L23, J19.

orde: sale; from *horridam* 'bristly', whence 'making one bristle'. Only the noun *ordure* survives.

psalm: 69 (Vg 68).

1:3:14   Mt27, Mk15, L23, J19.

forcenans: present participle of *forcener* 'to go mad', of which only the past participle *forcené* survives as an adjective.

mercy: in the old sense, as in English.

1:3:15   Mt27, Mk15, L23, J19.

quarré: carré; from *quadratum.*

iusqu'au dos du posteau (poteau): note onomatopoeia.

entenduë: shows concord by position. Likewise *renduë* later.

forging was forbidden: 'now there was no smith found throughout all the land of Israel: for the Philistines said, Lest the Hebrews make them swords or spears' (1 Samuel/Vg 1 Kings 13).

qui vous a d'en auoir . . .: qui vous a rendu la liberté d'en avoir.

altar stones: 'and there shalt thou build an altar unto the Lord thy God, an altar of stones: thou shalt not lift up any iron tool upon them' (Deuteronomy 27).

temple: 'and the house, when it was in building, was built of stone made ready before it was brought thither: so that there was neither hammer nor axe nor any tool of iron heard in the house' (1 Kings/Vg 3 Kings 6).

Tubal: Tubal-cain, 'an instructer of every artificer in brass and iron' (Genesis 4).

1:3:16   Mt27, Mk15, L23, J19.

elle n'y peut atteindre: elle ne peut y atteindre.

embas: en bas.

les bourreaux ont de mesme . . .: the poet could have written *les bourreaux à la corde ont de même recours;* his syntax and the clash of *corde/recours* are clearly enacting events.

oit: from *ouïr* (from *audire*); cf 'oyez!'

nerfs: covered almost anything that was not organ, muscle or bone.

1:3:18   Mt27, Mk15, L23, J19.

as he has foretold: 'they have pierced my hands and feet: they have numbered all my bones' (Psalm 22/Vg 21). This is the Vg reading; the Hebrew has 'like a lion (they are at) my hands and feet. I can count all my bones'; KJ combines elements of both. The Psalms are traditionally ascribed to David, who is traditionally an ancestor of Jesus. According to Mt and Mk, this was the psalm he quoted on the Cross ('My God, my God, why hast thou forsaken me?').

par tout: partout.

our circumcised: the Jews.

craignans: craignant.

rendit . . . fut dressée: rendît . . . fût dressée.

pour du creux preparé . . .: pour approcher le bout bas du creux préparé.

Cocyte: Cocytus, a river of Hades associated with lamentation.

1:3:19   Mt27, Mk15, L23, J19.

contenuës: shows concord by position.

craignez: craignant? Or an unconscious echo of 'neither fear ye the people of the land' (Numbers 14).

hé: such a colloquialism would have offended Classical taste.

r'attache: the *esbranlement* seems to make the crown of thorns bounce. The poet stresses that *ces exagerations . . . hors du texte des Euangelistes* are justified by the meditations of the Fathers, which lead one to believe that Jesus' killers *firent le plus sanglant pis (pire) dont ils peurent (purent) s'aduiser.*

1:3:20   Mt27, Mk15, L23, J19.

le va tantost . . .: va tantôt l'étendre dans le sépulcre. Pre-Classical (and Classical) French regularly places a pronoun object before a modal verb; cf *1:3:16 elle n'y peut atteindre.* Here *aller* is clearly seen as a modal verb.

Eurydice: because she was bitten by a snake and was rescued (at least for a time) from Hades by her husband, who was later torn to pieces.

fair one: the soul, following a Christian interpretation of the Song of Songs.

1:3:21   Mt27, Mk15, L23, J19.

fair one: see note to *1:3:20.*

semond: semonce.

pourtant: pour tant.

1:3:22

Deucalion: the Greek Noah.

motley bow . . . cloud: 'and God said . . . I do set my bow in the cloud, and it shall be for a token of a covenant between me and the earth . . . and the waters shall no more become a flood' (Genesis 9).

1:3:23

altar: 'and thou shalt make an altar to burn incense upon' (Exodus 30).

hypostasis: cf *substantia*.

pole: 'and Moses made a serpent of brass, and put it upon a pole, and it came to pass, that if a serpent had bitten any man, when he beheld the serpent of brass, he lived' (Numbers 21).

pense: *panse*.

winepress: the Cross, making wine from Christ the 'true vine' (J15), recalling the reproach against Israel as an unproductive vineyard (Isaiah 5). Christ is also identified as God who said 'I have trodden the winepress alone; and of the people there was none with me' (Isaiah 63), and Calvary as the new promised land where grapes grow (Numbers 13).

Jacob's ladder: 'and he dreamed, and behold a ladder set up on the earth, and the top of it reached to heaven: and behold the angels of God ascending and descending on it' (Genesis 28).

1:3:24

staff: with which Jacob crossed the Jordan (Genesis 32).

sword: with which David cut off Goliath's head (1 Samuel/Vg 1 Kings 17).

trident: the rod with which Moses parted the Red Sea (Exodus 14).

ost: 'army', from *hostem* 'enemy'; cf 'Lord God of hosts'.

wood: the Cross, recalling the tree with which Moses sweetened the bitter waters (Exodus 15).

accoisa: 'made *coi*', from *quietum*; cf *rester coi* 'to keep mum', and 'coy'.

singlez: *cinglez*.

1:3:25

n'aguere: the apostrophe recalls *n'(y) a guère* 'hardly any time ago'.

fair tower: the Cross seen as the beloved whose 'neck is like the tower of David builded for an armoury, whereon there hang a thousand bucklers, all shields of mighty men' (Song of Songs 4).

1:3:26

green wood: the tree of knowledge in the garden of Eden (Genesis 3).

dry wood: the Cross.

righteousness and peace . . .: quoting Psalm 85 (Vg 84).

1:3:27

saintly shepherd: Moses. 'And it came to pass, when Moses held up his hand, that Israel prevailed: and when he let down his hand, Amalek prevailed. But Moses' hands were heavy . . . and Aaron and Hur stayed up his hands' (Exodus 17).

poisle: *poêle*; cf 'pall'.

ialoux: cf 'zealous'.

par tout: *partout*.

1:3:29
This and the following two sonnets form a 'Cross' triptych.
Empyre: 'Empyrean', the outermost sphere of fire (*pyr*) and godhead in Ptolemaic cosmology.
this tree: the Cross.
bourbier: man was created, according to the Vg, from 'mud'; the Hebrew word also means KJ 'dust' (Genesis 2).
round machine: the universe. The Cross is the axle-tree on which the universe turns, 'the still point of the turning world'.

1:3:30
our three foes: the world, the flesh and the devil; a formula used in Counter-Reformation catechisms (and incorporated into Anglican prayer books), familiar enough for the poet not to comment on it.
nichans: nichant.
guindent: a favourite verb of the poet. His 'imitation' of the Passion Sunday hymn *Vexilla Regis* ends *Guidez nous, guindez nous au sublime repos*.

1:3:31
Orpheus: here simply a poet. For his correspondence with Christ, see *1:3:20*.
piteuse: 'full of pity'.
onques: jamais; from *unquam*.
those marked: 'and he called to the man . . . which had the writer's inkhorn by his side; and the Lord said unto him, Go through the midst of . . . Jerusalem, and set a mark upon the foreheads of the men that sigh and that cry for all the abominations that be done in the midst thereof. And to the others he said . . . Go ye . . . through the city, and smite' (Ezekiel 9). The 'mark' was a cross-shaped *tau*, the first letter of *torah* 'Law'.
coing: coin 'stamp, die' for striking coins.

1:3:61   J19.
Naomi: who after the death of her sons asked to be called not Naomi ('pleasant') but Mara ('bitter'; Ruth 1).
chetiue: 'wretched'.
griefues (grièves): from *graves*; only the adverb *grièvement* survives.
vieillard: Simeon.
Simeon: who sang the *Nunc dimittis* over the infant Jesus and predicted that Mary's soul would be pierced with a sword (L2).
martyre: tourment.

1:3:65   L23.
iournée: 'daylight'.
eut ailleurs detournée: eût (aurait) . . .; detournée shows concord by position.
veit: vit; spelt *veid* in *1:3:95, 1:3:100*.

1:3:77   Mt27, Mk15, J19.
impales a sponge: of the Evangelists the poet tends to favour J, who here says the sponge was 'put upon hyssop'. The poet's verb *enuironne* 'puts round' follows Vg *circumponentes*, which renders literally the Greek *perithentes*, though this can also mean 'putting on'. Hyssop (*hyssopos*) grows in a small bush, which was dipped in water and shaken for ritual sprinkling; cf 'purge me

with hyssop, and I shall be clean' (Psalm 51/Vg 50). Some translators compromise with 'hyssop stalk'; others emend the word to *hyssos* 'javelin' in the light of the 'reed' of Mt and Mk.

duly: the only known Jewish custom possible here is the ritual sprinkling, but the poet follows his Evangelist, who is probably recalling 'in my thirst they gave me vinegar to drink' (Psalm 69/Vg 68).

Old Man: Adam.

lord of lies: Satan.

qui vous la conuertie: *la* is *l'a*.

wild grapes: see note to *1:3:23* on 'winepress'.

1:3:78 J19.

au chaud mal: *mal* is a noun, to which *qui* refers.

au mourir: *au point de mourir*.

deut: *dut*.

did not eat: the Temptation (Mt4, L4).

sweated: the Agony (L4; cf *1:1:38*).

all is fulfilled: KJ has 'it is finished', but the poet is closer to Greek *tetelestai* and Vg *consummatum est*.

1:3:85 Mt27, Mk15, L23, J19.

into thy hands: quoted in the translation because the original refers to a sonnet not translated. According to L, Jesus quotes Psalm 31 (Vg 30).

the Fate: the goddess, hence death. The poet quotes Athanasius as saying that death dared not approach until it was summoned.

reaux: the poet's note respells the word *rehauts* and explains its source *en termes & langage des Peintres*.

ses temples sont crusées: *ses tempes sont creusées*.

tierce: *troisième*.

1:3:95 Mt27, Mk15, L23, J19.

Coronnel: *colonel*, a false etymology; cf 'admiral' from Arabic *amir*.

the leader of the Jews: Moses, who smote the rock (Exodus 17, Numbers 20).

Longinus: the traditional name of the Roman centurion who, seeing the earthquake that followed Jesus' death, declared him to be the Son of God (according to Mt and Mk; according to L, he called him a righteous man), thus becoming the first person – a gentile – to do so. The centurion is traditionally identified with the soldier who pierced Jesus' side with a spear (according to J).

plustost: *plus tôt*; the construction with *ne* is like *ne . . . guère*.

vn cristal: conventional term for clear water.

pus: Original Sin. The sestet demonstrates that the two chief sacraments of the Church – Baptism and the Eucharist – flow from the wounds of Christ.

1:3:96 Mt27, Mk15, L23, J19.

Jew: Joseph of Arimathea.

fidele . . . haste: the prosody shows that *fidele* qualifies the subject and that *haste* does not have a 'buffer' *h* as in *hâte*.

il ne s'en ose ouurir: *il n'ose s'en ouvrir* (i.e., *de sa sympathie*).

trespas . . . trépas: became the standard Classical euphemism; from *transpassum*.

descend: transitive.

lap: the poet reassures that though this is not scriptural, it is traditional under
the name *Pietà* and hence 'not indecent'.

1:3:97   J19.
This and the following three sonnets form a 'Mary Magdalen' triptych.
demeure froide: *garde son sang-froid*.
Sinner Saint: Mary Magdalen.

1:3:98
quelle voy-ie . . . cette face: *quelle est cette face que je vois*.
serene (sérène): *rend serein*.
pourpris: *enceinte*.
Venus' fires: votive lamps at Aphrodite's shrine in Cyprus.
massonnerent: *maçonnèrent*.
feet: recalling Jesus walking on the water (Mt14, Mk6, J6) and calming the storm
(Mt8, Mk4, L8).

1:3:99
more tears: recalling 'a woman in the city, which was a sinner', traditionally
identified with Mary Magdalen, who washed Jesus' feet with her tears (L7).
tandis: here an adverb, 'meanwhile'.
sabbath: begins at sunset on Friday.
ia: *déjà*.

1:3:100   Mt27, Mk15, L23, J19.
corruption: 'neither wilt thou suffer thy Holy One to see corruption'
(Psalm 16/Vg 15).
semon: *semons*.
ie vous puisse inhumer: *je puisse vous inhumer*.

2:1:1   Mt28, Mk16, L24, J20.
Styx: according to the Creeds, Christ between his death and resurrection
'descended into hell', where he freed the souls of the just who had died
before his coming.
comme: *comment*.
unopened tomb: that is, by human hand.
both his natures: human and divine.
son mespris: 'scorn of him'.
get up, girl: the elderly poet's homely invocation to Urania, the heavenly muse.

2:1:5
Coronnelles: here an adjective; see note to *1:3:95* on *Coronnel*.
open: the command, question and answer which form the rest of this sonnet
echo the 'lift up your heads, O ye gates' passage in Psalm 24 (Vg 23).
centre: hell was believed to be underground, so its abyss was at the centre of the
earth, the place furthest from the crystal sphere of heaven.

2:1:26
ver: the poet's note is about the silkworm (*ver à soie*). He also recalls Psalm 22
(Vg 21): 'I am a worm, and no man'.
pelican: an ancient belief, long since pressed into Christian service; cf the

pie pellicane, Jesu Domine of Thomas Aquinas' hymn *Adoro te devote* (translated by Crashaw) and the *petto del nostro Pellicano* of Dante (*Paradiso* 25). In a note the poet also quotes Psalm 102 (Vg 101): 'I am like a pelican of the wilderness', without attributing the simile to its being ritually unclean.

eagle: 'thy youth is renewed like the eagle's' (Psalm 103/Vg 102).

face: *fasse*.

2:1:35

phoenix: fabulous Ancient Egyptian bird which dies on a pyre of aromatic wood, the ashes producing its single offspring.

among the dead . . . free: 'I am as a man that hath no strength: free among the dead, like the slain that lie in the grave' (Psalm 88/Vg 87). A strenuous allusion, since the original context suggests 'free' in the sense of 'abandoned'.

2:1:43

Wheel: the Zodiac. The poet's astrology is purely poetic.

sa belle ame: Christ's.

rounded: the soul was thought to determine the body's shape before birth, so that physical beauty reflected inner goodness.

organe: sometimes used in pre-Classical French to mean 'body'.

Waterbearer: because Christians identify the 'man of sorrows' of Isaiah 53 with Jesus.

trassé: *tracé*.

feres: *bêtes sauvages*; from *feras*. The poet defends his usage by quoting Ronsard.

2:1:50

stag . . . river: an echo of 'as the hart panteth after the water brooks' (Psalm 42/ Vg 41), but the poet has other concerns.

hating the serpent: an ancient belief.

deuorée . . . asseruie: the former qualifies *mort*, the latter shows concord by position.

prophetic horn: the Psalmist's; see following note.

the Stag at Morn: for once the poet has gone beyond the Vg, and his researches into the Septuagint version and the Hebrew original of Psalm 22 (Vg 21, the 'Crucifixion' psalm) have revealed in the mysterious rubric 'for a morning capture' (*susceptione*) a reference to a hind. Since the hunted beast is clearly Christ he offers 'a thousand songs of praise' and adapts its sex to his purpose. (As KJ indicates in a marginal gloss, leaving the Hebrew untranslated, the rubric is an instruction to sing the psalm to a tune called 'The Hind of the Morning'.)

compliment: *éloge*.

2:1: Vœu pour la fin de ce Liure 'Prayer to end this Book'

intelligible: but not perceptible; that is, accessible to the mind but not to the senses.

sphere: the original 'intelligible sphere', says the poet, was the planet Mercury, associated with Hermes Trismegistus, the mythical inventor of alchemy; the term is applied to Christ because he too is 'thrice greatest' as philosopher, high priest and king.

your centre is everywhere: the poet acknowledges Diodorus Siculus (1st century BC) as his source, but it was Empedocles (5th century BC) who first

116

described God as 'a circle whose centre is everywhere and whose circumference is nowhere'.

par tout: *partout*.

your surface: Christ's body.

qu'il passe: *l'Amour*.

2:2:64   L24, J20.

he lives: previous sonnets, not translated, tell of Christ's appearances after his resurrection.

the fourth: taste, by eating before his disciples.

the fifth: smell, by breathing on them.

whale: the poet mentions Aquinas as the source of this unlikely information.

cêt haim: *ce haim*.

curée: parts of a stag given to the hounds, whence 'quarry'; from *cuirée* 'skinful'.
    Faire curée is 'to make a meal' of e.g. someone's reputation, to tear it to shreds.

soüefue (souève): 'sweet', from *suavem*. The popular form *souef* (cf Italian *soave*) has since been overtaken by the learned *suave*; cf note to *1:2:63* on *Carmes*.

2:3:11   Mk16, L24, A1.

empyrée: see note to *1:3:29* on *Empyre*.

gigante: *l'herbe* (the poet glosses) *dicte autrement solaire, pource qu'elle suit le Soleil appellée par plusieurs Gigante à cause qu'elle s'éleue par dessus les autres plantes d'vne extreme hauteur.* He lists it in his index under *heliotropium*.

Nerée: Nereus, the Old Man of the Sea, patron of the Aegean.

2:3:25

pourroy: *pourrais*.

cornetts: 'little horns', blown like trumpets and fingered like recorders, popular with angels in stained glass windows.

liesse: *joie*; from *laetitiam*.

all the just: rescued from limbo during the harrowing of hell.

snowy head . . . fireballs: 'his head and his hairs were white like wool, as white as snow; and his eyes were as a flame of fire' (Revelation 1).

2:4:1   A2.

La Ceppède: the poet signs off, invoking the Holy Spirit direct.

apris: *appris*, *habile*. The original punctuation of this sonnet is misleading; it is best read as a single sentence (of which Mallarmé would have approved) thus: lines 1-2 invocation, line 3 first petition (*dardez* . . .), line 4 second petition (*rendez* . . .), specified in lines 5-11 (*non pas pour . . . mais bien pour . . .*) with a disclaimer in parenthesis (*j'esquiue . . . dépeches*), line 12 third petition (*secondez* . . .), lines 12-14 fourth petition (*façonnez* . . .).

j'esquiue: the original Germanic verb was used of paring leather and grinding gems; cf 'skive, shave'. The French verb means by extension 'to dodge' e.g. a blow in combat ('a close shave') or uncongenial work; cf Spanish *esquivar*, Italian *schivare*.

prêches: *prêche* 'Protestant sermon', used mockingly by Catholics (as here) of any long, abstruse discourse.

Procession: the Nicene (not, as the poet says, the Apostles') Creed asserted in the 4th century that the Holy Spirit 'proceedeth from the Father'. The Western addition in the 5th century of the word *Filioque* 'and from the Son' was resisted by Rome until the 9th century, whereupon Byzantium excommunicated Rome for corrupting the faith: this was a major cause of the Great Schism between East and West in the 11th century. Despite his disclaimer, the poet airs the controversy afresh in a note on the need to distinguish Generation (Father to Son) and Procession (Father to Holy Spirit), thus unwittingly showing his support of the Eastern position.

dépeches: a diplomatic (and military) term, used diplomatically here to offset the boldness of *prêches*.

folk of the unlearned kind: before reflecting on the immense erudition that has nevertheless gone into the *Theorems*, it is worth recalling the poet's description of the work in his Foreword as a child 'bearing in his hand the book of the Prophet . . . written within for the learned and without for the ignorant'; see note to Foreword on 'Prophet'.

comme: comment.

estez: *êtes*? Following *z* marked a tonic *e*; this must be a misprint for either *estes* or (less probably) *estiez*.

2:4:6   A2.

aussi: the previous sonnet, not translated, speaks of the gifts of the Spirit.

hypostatiquement: see note to *1:3:23* on 'hypostasis'. The poet hastens to reassure doubters of his orthodoxy that God is not embodied in *cête vehemence* as in the person of Christ.

le seul Verbe a faict cête accointance: *le Verbe (de Dieu) a seul fait ce contact* ('acquaintance').

progez: a curiously medieval spelling of *projet*, here 'carrying out'.

2:4:7   A2.

Third Person: of the Trinity.

soft whispers: recalling Elijah's flight from God, who sent a wind, an earthquake, a fire, 'and after the fire a still small voice' (1 Kings/Vg 3 Kings 19).

ventelet: a double diminutive.

écharsement: 'sparingly'; cf 'scarcely'.

marquat: marquât.

2:4:9   A2.

St Luke: the author of Acts. This sonnet is a gloss on one word in verse 3: 'and there appeared unto them cloven tongues like as of fire, and it sat upon each of them'. KJ 'cloven' does not take in all of the Greek *diamerizomenai* and the Vg *dispertitae*, both of which mean 'divided' in many senses. The poet, on behalf of his Church (and later translators), prefers the less vivid interpretation, doubtless in the light of St Paul's words on 'diversities of gifts' in 1 Corinthians 12, the conclusion of which in the famous chapter that follows is that love is the most important gift of all.

feal: fidèle; both from *fidelem*.

tout par tout: a reinforced *partout*; cf *ià desia* in *1:1:21*.

Babel: where a tower (probably a pagan *ziggurat*) was built to reach heaven till God confounded the language of the builders (Genesis 11). Pentecost is traditionally regarded as a reversal of Babel.

2:4:11   A2.

à soy: à lui-même.

our eleven: the poet has overlooked the appointment (A1) of a twelfth apostle to replace Judas Iscariot.

Olympus' secretaries: the Evangelists.

2:4:14   A2.

si: *au contraire*.

that draw this Spirit: recalling Psalm 119 (Vg 118), section *pe*.

KJ follows the Hebrew closely ('I opened my mouth, and panted') but the Vg has *et attraxi spiritum* 'and I drew breath' – or, for present purposes, 'and I attracted the Spirit'.

celle: *la fumée*.

2:4:17   A2.

this Potter: the poet attributes the metaphor to Paul (Romans 9), who doubtless had in mind 'behold, as the clay is in the potter's hand, so are ye in mine hand, O house of Israel' (Jeremiah 18).

hot Gospel's kiln: a delightful coincidence. The poet's heretical English contemporaries, the Puritans, were derisively called Hot Gospellers on account of their zeal. The expression has since become even less respectable.

2:4:23   A2.

some say: the poet is disagreeing with scholars who attributed the diversity of languages to the richness of Adam's vocabulary, a view which undermines the myth of Babel and hence Pentecost itself; see note to *2:4:9* on 'Babel'.

aux langages diuers: *aux langues diverses*.

soint: *soient*.

que la superbe obscur auoit rendu: *que l'orgueil avait rendu obscur*.

Heber: or Eber, a descendant of Noah (Genesis 10), after whom the language and its speakers are named. (It was the name proposed for his son by Eliezer Ben-Yehuda, the pioneer of modern Hebrew, but rejected because no one had heard of it.)

Zephaniah: 'therefore wait ye upon me, saith the Lord, until the day that I rise up to the prey . . . for then will I turn to the people a pure language, that they may all call upon the name of the Lord' (Zephaniah 3).

seiour: *séjour permanent*.

Index